A
FIRST
THESAURUS

The Word Hunter's Companion

JAMES GREEN

Assisted by Arthur Thomas

MODERN CURRICULUM PRESS

© IRWIN PUBLISHING, INC., 1977
Toronto, Canada

Developed from The Word Hunter's Companion
© Basil Blackwell, 1976

ISBN 0-8136-1993-9 Paperback
ISBN 0-8136-1992-0 Hardcover

MODERN CURRICULUM PRESS

A Division of Simon & Schuster
13900 Prospect Road Cleveland Ohio 44136

10 9 8 7 6 5   93 92

The reconstructed Treasury of the Athenians
at Delphi, Greece

A FIRST THESAURUS

Many hundreds of years ago when some of the city states of
Ancient Greece were beginning to grow rich, their rulers and
chief men had to provide safe places to store the cities' treas-
ures. In those days banks had not been invented, but the rulers
of the cities built treasure houses to store the gold and precious
things. These treasure houses were often built near important
temples, where no one would dare to displease the gods by
disturbing them. There the treasure could be kept safe for its

owners. The Greeks called such a treasure house *thesauros*. This word comes from a Greek verb which means "to put," and at first it probably meant only "storeroom" or "storehouse," but later it came to mean "treasury." The Romans changed the spelling to *thesaurus* and kept the meaning "treasury." Today we use *thesaurus* to mean a "treasury of words," or, a "treasury of knowledge."

Since words are powerful tools for expressing thoughts and directing actions, for broadening knowledge, for creating new processes and for achieving satisfying aims, we all need a rich and varied treasury of words. This book can help you to create such a treasury for yourself.

How to Use a Thesaurus

When you are writing it is sometimes difficult to find or to remember the word which will say exactly what you mean, and you may use a word which does not precisely express your thought. Or you may want to make your writing more interesting by using a number of words which have similar meanings instead of repeating the same word over and over.

In this book there are numbered words in *bold type* called "key words." These are probably words you use very often. Underneath each key word is a list of words that have the same meaning or similar meanings. These meanings are explained so that you should be able to choose exactly the word you need to make your meaning precise or to vary your vocabulary.

Use the index at the end of the book to find the word you were thinking of using, then look up the number given beside it and choose what you think is the best word for your purpose.

CONTENTS

NOUNS

1   all

everybody   All people.
everyone   All people.
everything   All things.
the entire   The whole amount, complete with nothing missing.
the sum   All the parts added together.
the total   The full amount.
the whole   All together with nothing missing; the sum of all the parts.

2   animal

amphibian   A creature able to live on land and in water.
beast   Any four-legged animal.
bird   A feathered creature with wings.
creature   Any person or animal, living or dead.
fish   A creature living in water and breathing through gills.
insect   A small six-legged creature with its body in three parts.
mammal   An animal which suckles its young.
monster   An unusually large and terrifying creature.
pet   A tame creature kept for pleasure.
reptile   A scaly, cold-blooded creature which creeps on very short legs or on its belly.
rodent   An animal with front teeth especially suited for gnawing.
vermin   (a) Small, unpleasant animals which harm crops or prey on game.
(b) Insects that are body parasites, such as fleas, lice, bedbugs. [Notice that 'vermin' is always plural.]

3   answer

excuse   An explanation to avoid blame.
explanation   A statement making something clear.
rejoinder   An answer to a reply.
reply   Something said, written or done in answer.
response   (a) A reply.
(b) A reaction.
retort   An answer flung back at once.
riposte   (a) A fencer's quick thrust following a parry.
(b) A quick sharp reply.
solution   (a) The solving of a problem.
(b) An explanation of a problem.

4 baby

brat An unruly child

cherub (a) An angel usually pictured as a beautiful, winged baby.

(b) A happy baby with chubby cheeks like those of a cherub.

child A person who is older than a baby and younger than an adolescent.

infant A baby. A very young child.

toddler A small child who walks with short unsteady steps.

tot A very small child.

5 bag

briefcase A flat case mostly used for carrying papers.

duffel bag A large bag of canvas or heavy cloth used by campers, hikers, soldiers to carry personal belongings.

handbag A woman's small case for carrying money, keys, cosmetics.

haversack A canvas bag with straps, used by hikers to carry food.

holdall A cloth traveling case.

knapsack A canvas or leather bag for carrying clothes or equipment on the back.

portfolio A briefcase for carrying loose papers, drawings.

purse A woman's handbag.

rucksack A canvas bag carried on the back with straps over both shoulders.

sack A large bag of coarse cloth.

saddlebag A bag carried across a horse or at the back of a bicycle.

schoolbag A leather or plastic case used by schoolchildren to carry books.

suitcase A case used for carrying clothes.

6 ball

globe A round object.

orb A ball shaped object. A globe; a sphere.

sphere A ball shaped object. A globe.

7 boat

canoe A narrow, lightweight boat with both ends pointed, generally moved by paddling.

7 boat (con't.)

    coaster A cargo boat which travels along the coast.

    craft A boat, ship or aircraft.

    dinghy (a) A small rowboat.

        (b) A ship's small boat.

        (c) A small sailboat.

    ferryboat A boat used to carry goods or people across a river or narrow stretch of water.

    galleon A large ancient sailing ship of several decks with high bow and stern.

    galley An ancient ship moved by oars and sails, often worked by slaves or convicts.

    launch A motor-driven boat used for pleasure or patrol.

    schooner A fore-and-aft rigged vessel usually with two or three masts.

    submarine A vessel designed to travel on or below the surface of the sea.

    tender A small vessel attending a larger one.

    trawler A fishing boat which drags a net along the bottom of the sea.

    tug A small powerful boat used to tow other boats.

    vessel A large boat. A ship.

    yacht (a) A light sailing vessel especially designed for racing.

        (b) A powered luxury vessel built for pleasure cruising.

8 book

    album (a) A book with blank pages in which a collection of items may be formed.

        (b) A collection of printed music or pictures in book form.

    anthology A collection of writings by various authors.

    atlas A collection of maps.

    classic A work of literature of lasting merit.

    diary (a) A book prepared for making day-to-day records.

        (b) An account of the day-to-day life of the writer.

    dictionary A collection of words in alphabetical order, with their meanings.

    encyclopedia A work, in one or more volumes, giving information about many subjects.

    handbook A convenient book of instructions.

    log A daily record of events, especially those on a sea voyage.

    manual A small book of instructions or explanation.

8 book (con't.)

manuscript (a) Typed or written work which an author sends to a publisher.

(b) A handwritten book sometimes decorated.

novel An invented story of people and events, long enough to fill one or more volumes.

paperback A book with paper covers.

publication A printed book, magazine or paper issued in quantity.

textbook A book of instruction dealing with a particular subject or study in school or college.

thesaurus (a) A treasury. A storehouse.

(b) A dictionary of synonyms.

thriller An exciting book; a story of crime, detection or mystery.

tome A very heavy book, often old or dull.

volume (a) A book.

(b) A book forming part of a set or series.

9   box

cabinet A cupboard made of wood or metal, and sometimes glass, often used for display.

caddy A metal or plastic container for storing tea.

carton A cardboard container.

case A container with glass, leather or wooden sides that protects items inside.

casket (a) A small box of fine workmanship used to hold jewelry or trinkets.

(b) A coffin.

chest A large wooden box with a hinged lid, sometimes bound with metal straps.

container Any article in which something can be held.

crate A large wooden container used to protect goods in transit.

locker A box or small cupboard usually fitted with a lock.

safe A metal container with strong locks for storing valuables.

strongbox A metal box which can be securely locked for storing valuables.

trunk A box of wood or metal with a hinged lid, used for traveling.

10   boy

adolescent A person between childhood and adulthood.

10 boy (con't.)

child   Someone older than a baby but not yet grown up.

juvenile   A young person.

lad   A boy. A youth.

minor   A person under the age of 18.

schoolboy   A boy who attends school.

stripling   A thin young man. A youth.

teen-ager   A person aged over 12 but not yet 20.

urchin   (a) A mischievous boy.

   (b) A poor boy of ragged appearance.

youngster   A young person; a teen-ager.

youth   A young man.

11   bus

motorcoach   A single-deck passenger vehicle.

streetcar   A public vehicle driven by electricity along rails in a road.

trolley   A bus powered by electricity from overhead cables.

12   car

automobile   A car.

convertible   A car with a roof which can be put up and taken down.

coupé   A closed two-seater car.

hearse   A large funeral vehicle used for carrying the coffin.

jalopy   An old car in poor condition.

jeep   A strong open vehicle developed by the U.S. armed forces for rough ground.

limousine   A large, luxury motor car.

race car   A very powerful car designed especially for racing.

sedan   A car with fixed roof and sides for more than two people.

sports car   A fast powerful car designed for road use.

taxi   A car with driver available for hire.

13   chair

armchair   A chair with supports for the arms.

bench   A long seat without arms or back, usually made of wood.

couch   A long, low upholstered seat on which to sit or lie.

deck chair   A collapsible canvas or plastic chair with a wooden or metal frame.

lawn chair   An outdoor chair similar to a deck chair.

13 chair (con't.)

pew A long wooden seat with back and arms for members of a church congregation.

rocking chair A chair designed to rock backward and forward.

seat Anything to sit on.

settee An upholstered seat for two or more persons.

settle A long, high-backed wooden seat.

sofa A long upholstered couch with back and arms.

stool A backless seat for one person.

throne The ceremonial chair for a king or other person of high rank.

14 city

borough A self-governing, incorporated town.

metropolis The chief city in a country or region.

port A city or town with a harbor.

suburb An outlying part of a town or city.

town A municipality with more people than a village, but fewer than a city.

15 coat

cloak A long, loose outer garment draped from the shoulders.

jacket A short coat.

overcoat A long coat worn out of doors over indoor clothing.

parka A heavy, hooded outer jacket.

raincoat A lightweight waterproof overcoat.

16 crowd

audience A group of people gathered to hear or see.

bunch A group of people. [Informal.]

congregation A group of people gathered for a religious service.

crush A tightly packed mass of people.

galaxy (a) A great number of stars forming one system.
(b) A brilliant or splendid group.

group A number of people sharing interests, views, social customs or beliefs.

horde A very large group.

host A very large crowd or army.

huddle A confused, closely packed group.

16 crowd (con't.)

mob   A lawless and excited crowd.

multitude   A very great number of people.

rabble   A disorderly crowd. A mob.

throng   A large, closely packed crowd.

17   drink

mouthful   Enough to fill the mouth.

nightcap   A drink taken before going to bed at night.

sip   A small quantity taken by the lips.

swig   A hearty drink. [Informal.]

taste   A very small quantity.

toast   A drink in honor of someone or something.

18   farm

market garden   Agricultural land used for the commerical production of fruit and vegetables.

ranch   A very large farm mainly for grazing cattle.

spread   A ranch.

19   fight

affray   A scrambling untidy outbreak of fighting.

battle   A large-scale fight between military forces.

blitz   A sudden violent attack.

campaign   A connected series of military operations planned to achieve a particular result.

combat   A struggle between two people or two forces.

conflict   A violent disagreement between sides.

dogfight   A fight between enemy warplanes chasing and dodging each other.

duel   A combat between two persons.

feud   A persistent quarrel leading to outbreaks of fighting often between families or clans.

melee   A confused fight at close quarters.

scrap   A small unplanned fight.

scrimmage   A rough fight or struggle.

scuffle   A small, untidy, confused struggle.

skirmish   A hasty fight between small groups from two rival forces.

tussle   A struggle. A scuffle.

war   A major struggle between nations or groups of nations.

20 fire

beacon   A signal-fire on high ground.
blaze   A fire burning furiously.
bonfire   (a) A garden fire for burning rubbish.
  (b) An outdoor fire built for celebration.
conflagration   A large destructive fire.
flame   A tongue of fire.
flare   A brief blaze of fire.
holocaust   (a) An offering that is entirely burned.
  (b) Complete consumption or destruction by fire.

21 friend

acquaintance   A person whom one knows slightly.
ally   Someone who supports and cooperates in a plan of action.
associate   A companion or partner. A fellow worker.
chum   A close friend. [Informal.]
colleague   An associate in a profession.
companion   Someone who spends much time in the company of another.
comrade   A close companion and supporter.
crony   An old close friend.
fan   An admirer of a notable person. [Informal.]
neighbor   Someone who lives near.
partner   Someone who shares in an activity or undertaking on an equal basis.
patron   Someone who gives his approval and support to a person or cause.

22 game

competition   A test of skill or strength between contestants.
contest   A test of skill or strength between contestants.
event   One of the parts of a competition.
match   A competition between two equal sides.
rally   A large meeting.
sport   A form of amusement or play. A game.
tournament   (a) A series of contests often taking several days.
  (b) A medieval contest of arms.

23 garden

flower garden   A garden for growing flowers.
garden patch   A small garden.

23 garden (con't.)

market garden A garden in which produce is grown for sale.
orchard A collection of fruit trees.
plot A small piece of land on which fruit, flowers or vegetables are grown.
vegetable garden A garden for growing vegetables for a household.

24 girl

adolescent A person between childhood and adulthood.
child Someone older than a baby but not yet grown up.
damsel A young girl; a maiden. [Poetic.]
juvenile A young person.
lass A young girl.
lassie A young girl.
minor A person not yet 18.
schoolgirl A girl attending school.
teen-ager A person aged over 12 but not yet 20.
tomboy A young girl who is rough and boylike in her behavior.
youngster A young person; a teen-ager.

25 help

aid Help; support.
assistance Help; support; aid.
comfort Encouragement and sympathy, especially in sorrow.
protection Defense from harm.
reinforcement The addition of strength.
relief The removal or lessening of need, anxiety or pain.
rescue The act of saving from danger.
service A helpful act. Help; aid.
support Cooperative assistance; help; aid.

26 horse

cart horse A sturdy horse able to pull heavy loads.
colt A young male horse.
filly A young female horse.
foal A newborn horse.
hunter A strong horse used for cross-country riding.
mare A fully-grown female horse.
mount A horse for riding.
pony A horse of a small breed, usually not more than 14 hands high.

26 horse (con't.)

racehorse   A horse bred or kept for racing.

saddle horse   A horse for riding.

stallion   A fully-grown male horse, especially one kept for breeding.

thoroughbred   A horse bred from a long line of good ancestors.

27   house

apartment   A set of rooms forming a complete home on one floor of a larger building.

bungalow   A cottage.

castle   A fortified residence or stronghold dating from the medieval period.

cottage   (a) A small house.
(b) A small house for vacation use.

lodge   A small house, especially for vacation use.

maisonette   A self-contained apartment on more than one floor.

manse   A dwelling.

mansion   A large imposing residence.

palace   A large and splendid house, usually the home of a monarch, bishop or nobleman.

parsonage   Dwelling provided by a church.

prefab   A house made from preassembled units.

rectory   A clergyman's house.

shack   A small, roughly-built house.

28   island

atoll   A ring-shaped coral island.

isle   A small island. An island.

islet   A very small island.

29   job

assignment   A task given to somebody.

chore   A routine, often unenjoyable task.

employment   An occupation by which a person earns a living. Work.

errand   A task someone is sent to do.

mission   Special work someone is sent to do.

29 job (con't.)

occupation The work by which someone earns his living.

profession An occupation which requires higher education and specialized training.

situation A place to work; a job.

task A piece of work. A duty.

vocation An occupation or profession, particularly one which a person feels strongly impelled to follow.

work (a) The effort of doing or making something.

(b) Occupation; job.

30 land

continent A very large unbroken area of land usually containing several countries.

country (a) A land inhabited by one nation, with definite political boundaries and a name.

(b) Land away from towns or cities.

county An area of land smaller than a state, designated for purposes of government.

district A small area or locality.

estate A large piece of land belonging to a person.

island A piece of land surrounded by water.

mainland The larger part of a continent or country, apart from islands nearby.

parish A neighborhood diocese.

province A large area of a country divided for purposes of government.

region An area of land with common features.

state (a) The territory of a government.

(b) A large area of a country divided for purposes of government.

territory Region; area of land.

31 light

brilliance An intense brightness.

daylight The light of day.

dazzle A bewildering brightness.

flare A bright blaze of light sometimes used as a signal or target-marker.

flash A sudden short burst of light.

glare A fierce, bright light.

31 light (con't.)

gleam   A short flash of light. A faint light.
glimmer   A faint wavering light.
glint   A gleam; a flash.
glitter   A bright sparkling light.
gloss   A superficial luster of brightness.
glow   A steady light.
illumination   Light. Lighting up; making bright.
luster   A bright shine on the surface. Brightness.
moonlight   The light from the moon.
phosphorescence   The luminous appearance of substances that give off light at temperatures lower than burning.
radiance   A light shining in bright rays.
sparkle   Light sent out in little sparks. Glitter.
sunlight   The light from the sun.
sunshine   Bright sunlight.

32   lot

abundance   A plentiful supply over and above what is necessary.
host   A very large crowd or army.
multitude   A very great number, especially of people.
profusion   A very great number. An abundance.

33   love

affection   A friendly feeling; fondness. Love.
devotion   A deep enduring affection.
fondness   Liking; affection.
friendship   A feeling of affection between friends.
passion   A strong, sometimes uncontrolled love.
regard   A feeling of kindly respect.
tenderness   A kind, sometimes protective, feeling.

34   meal

banquet   An elaborate meal eaten on a special occasion.
barbecue   An outdoor meal roasted or smoked over a charcoal fire.
feast   An abundant meal eaten on a joyful occasion.
picnic   A meal eaten outdoors using food previously packed.
repast   A meal.
snack   (a) A light meal.
          (b) A small amount of food eaten between meals.
spread   A feast. [Informal.]

35 money

bill A piece of paper money.
bullion Gold or silver bars.
cash Money; coins and bills.
coinage Money in the form of coins.
currency Money in use in a country.
finances Money; funds; revenues.
funds A supply or source of money.
riches A plentiful supply of money or valuables.
wealth A plentiful supply of money or riches.

36 mountain

crest A ridge, peak or summit of a mountain.
hill An area of raised ground not as high as a mountain.
peak The pointed top of a mountain or high hill.
ridge A long narrow top or crest of land.
summit The highest point or top of a mountain or hill.

37 noise

bang A loud sudden noise.
call A cry or shout.
creak A loud squeak. A grating sound.
cry (a) A loud sound expressing emotion or feeling,
     (b) The call of an animal or bird.
howl A long, loud wavering cry.
murmur A low, indistinct drawn-out sound.
roar A loud deep sound.
scream A high-pitched cry.
screech A long, harsh piercing sound.
shriek A high-pitched cry.
sound A noise.
squeak A short, sharp grating sound.
tap The sound of a light blow.
thud A heavy sound of a blow or fall.
wail A long cry of grief or pain.
whimper A low broken cry.
whine A repeated, low complaining cry.

38 people

brotherhood A close group who share a common interest or
     aim.
clan A group of related families.

38 people (con't.)

community   (a) The people of any district or municipality.
(b) A number of people who live together and share the same interests and laws.

folk   All men, women and children in a given area or community.

humanity   All men, women and children everywhere.

mankind   All human beings.

nation   The people of one country.

persons   Individual people.

population   All the persons living in a particular area.

public   The people in general.

race   A major group of mankind who have certain physical characteristics in common.

society   A number of people, forming a group, having the same interests or purpose.

tribe   A group of people sharing the same customs and beliefs.

39   picture

cartoon   A comic drawing.

collage   A picture made by sticking many different things to a surface.

diagram   A line drawing explaining something.

drawing   A picture made in crayon, pen-and-ink or pencil.

fresco   A picture painted on the plaster of a wall.

illustration   A picture showing a scene in a book or play.

landscape   A picture of natural inland scenery.

mosaic   A picture made up of small colored pieces of the same material fixed close together.

mural   A picture painted on a wall.

old master   A picture painted by a great artist of the past.

photograph   A picture produced by a camera.

portrait   A picture of a person.

poster   A picture advertising some product or event.

print   A reproduction of an original picture.

representation   A likeness; a picture.

silhouette   A picture in profile done in a dark color against a light background.

sketch   A rough draft for a picture.

40 price

charge   The price asked for something.

cost   The price paid for something.

estimate   The forecast of a price.

fare   The cost of a journey.

fee   The sum paid to a professional person for service or advice.

quotation   A statement naming a price or estimate.

rate   A price, usually of a utility or service.

retail price   The price at which something is sold to the public.

tariff   A list of duties or taxes on imports and exports.

value   The amount someone would expect to pay for something.

wholesale price   The price charged by the manufacturer to the storekeeper or retailer.

41 rain

cloudburst   A sharp downfall of very heavy rain likely to cause flooding.

deluge   A long, very heavy rainfall usually causing flooding.

downpour   A heavy fall of rain.

drizzle   Very fine rain.

monsoon   Very strong wind accompanied by steady rain during the wet season in some tropical countries.

thunderstorm   Heavy rain with thunder and lightning.

42 rest

remainder   That which is left.

remnant   A small remaining part.

residue   What is left after a part is taken. Remainder.

surplus   What is left over and above what is necessary; an extra amount left over.

43 road

alley   A narrow passage between buildings.

avenue   A wide street often bordered by trees.

blind alley   An alley closed at one end.

bypass   A road built for fast traffic to avoid a city or town.

byroad   A side road with little traffic.

causeway   A raised road or path, generally over shallow water.

43 road (con't.)

cul-de-sac   An alley or road closed at one end.

driveway   A private road from the street to a house.

highway   A main road.

lane   A narrow strip of road.

path   A pedestrian way.

route   A course or road chosen in traveling.

side road   A road that is not a main road.

street   A road lined with buildings.

44   sea

deep   (a) A deep part of the sea.

(b) Any part of the sea very far from land.

high seas   The open ocean.

main   The open sea; the ocean.

ocean   A widespread area of sea.

45   ship

aircraft carrier   A ship that carries aircraft.

clipper   A sailing ship built and rigged for speed.

craft   A boat, ship or aircraft.

destroyer   A small fast warship fitted with guns, torpedoes and other weapons.

frigate   (a) A three-masted warship of medium size.

(b) A modern warship smaller than a destroyer.

liner   A ship belonging to a transportation system.

man-of-war   A warship.

merchantman   A ship used in commerce.

submarine   A ship designed to operate on or below the surface of the sea.

tanker   A ship with tanks for carrying liquid freight.

46   shop

bazaar   (a) An Eastern market.

(b) A short sale of goods to raise money for a particular cause.

department store   A large store selling many types of goods.

kiosk   A small, light building with one or more sides open, used to sell newspaper, magazines and candy.

market   An open space or public building where goods are sold from stalls.

46 shop (con't.)

    mart A market.

    newsstand A small, light structure used to sell newspapers.

    self-service store A store in which customers serve themselves.

    stall A table or stand displaying goods for sale.

    store An establishment where goods are sold to the public.

    supermarket A large self-service store where groceries and household supplies are sold.

47   shore

    beach The low-lying land at the water's edge.

    coast A stretch of land bordering the sea or a large area of water.

    lakefront The land along the edge of a lake.

    seashore The beach at the sea's edge.

    strand A shore. [Poetic.]

48   sleep

    catnap A short light sleep often taken sitting down.

    doze A light sleep.

    forty winks A short sleep.

    hibernation A natural sleep of some animals throughout the winter.

    nap A short sleep taken during the day.

    siesta A midday sleep taken in hot countries.

    slumber Sleep. [Poetic.]

    snooze Sleep; doze; nap. [Informal.]

49   story

    account A connected story of events.

    anecdote A short, often funny, account of an incident.

    autobiography A person's life story written by himself.

    biography A person's life story written by someone else.

    chronicle A record of events usually in strict order of time.

    description An account setting out a picture in words.

    diary A day-to-day record of events.

    fable A short story made up to teach a lesson.

    fairy tale A tale of magical events and fairies.

    fantasy An imaginative tale.

    folk tale A story passed down from the remote past by word of mouth.

49 story (con't.)

history A record of past events showing their special
importance.

legend A story of gods or heroes handed down from the past
by word of mouth and possibly having some basis in
fact.

memoirs A book based on one person's memories.

myth A traditional or legendary story usually dealing with
gods or heroes and often trying to account for
something in nature.

narrative A story of events or experiences.

novel A book-length story about imaginary people or events.

parable A short story meant to teach a lesson about life.

report A detailed account of an event or situation.

romance A pleasant imaginary love story.

saga A long account of gods and heroes.

serial A story told in several parts at intervals.

statement A simple bare account.

tale A story; a narrative.

thriller A sensational story usually dealing with crime, detection or mystery. [Informal.]

yarn A long drawn-out story often hard to believe and usually told aloud. [Informal.]

50 teacher

coach An instructor who prepares a person for an examination or sport.

governess A lady who teaches young children in their home.

guru A Hindu teacher of meditation or religious wisdom.

instructor A teacher.

lecturer (a) Someone who delivers talks.
(b) A teacher in a college or university, who does
not have tenure.

principal A head of a school.

professor A teacher of the highest rank in a university
department.

tutor A teacher who gives lessons to one person or a very
small group.

51 thief

bandit An armed robber.

blackmailer Someone who demands money by threatening to
make public unpleasant secrets.

51 thief (con't.)

brigand An armed robber.

burglar Someone who forces an entry into a house in order to steal.

embezzler Someone who dishonestly uses money entrusted to him.

footpad A highway robber who goes on foot.

highwayman An armed horseman who robs travelers.

kidnapper Someone who seizes and holds a person by force.

kleptomaniac A person who has uncontrollable impulses to steal.

pickpocket A person who steals from people's pockets.

pilferer Someone who steals in small amounts.

pirate Someone living by robbery at sea.

poacher A person who catches fish or game on another man's land without permission.

robber Someone who steals by threats or force.

shoplifter Someone who steals goods in stores.

swindler Someone who cheats or defrauds.

52 top

apex The top; the peak.

brow The top edge of a steep cliff or hill.

crest The topmost point or edge.

crown The top; the highest part.

peak A pointed mountaintop.

pinnacle The highest pointed part of a mountain or building.

summit The highest point.

zenith (a) The point in the heavens directly overhead.
(b) The highest point.

53 war

Armageddon A great and final conflict.

campaign A connected series of military operations planned to achieve a particular result.

conflict A prolonged struggle. A fight.

crusade (a) A military expedition of the medieval age intended to bring the Holy Land under Christian control.
(b) A war with a religious purpose.

53 war (con't.)

guerrilla war   Irregular warfare carried out by small, armed bands.

hostilities   Any acts of war.

strife   Vigorous or bitter conflict.

total war   A war in which the whole population is attacked.

54   wood

bush   A wooded area.

forest   An extensive area of land covered with trees.

grove   A group of trees.

plantation   A group of trees planted by man.

scrub   Low, stunted trees or shrubs.

thicket   A dense growth of shrubs or trees.

underbrush   Bushes and small trees growing under large trees in a forest.

woodland   Wooded country.

woodlot   A small area of trees forming part of a farm.

55   zoo

aquarium   (a) a container in which fish and other water animals are kept.

(b) a building containing a collection of glass-sided tanks for fish and other water animals.

aviary   A large cage for keeping birds.

menagerie   A collection of animals exhibited in captivity.

vivarium   A place for keeping live animals so that they may be easily observed.

wildlife park   A park where animals are kept and exhibited in the open.

ADJECTIVES

56 big

ample Large; extensive; roomy; more than enough; abundant.

bulky Taking up much space. So large that it is awkward to handle.

colossal Huge; gigantic; vast.

considerable Quite a lot. Great; much.

elephantine Like an elephant. Huge; heavy.

enormous Very much larger than usual.

extensive Spreading over a large area.

fat Overweight.

gigantic As big as a giant.

great Big; large; important.

huge Very much larger than usual.

hulking Big and clumsy.

immense Very much larger than usual.

king-sized Larger or longer than is usual for its kind. [Informal.]

large Big; extensive.

mammoth Huge; gigantic.

massive Large, heavy and impressive.

mountainous Huge.

spacious Having much space; roomy.

stout Somewhat overweight, but not fat.

vast Covering enormous space.

57 boring

dull Lacking variety or interest.

humdrum Commonplace; dull; without variety.

irksome Tiresome; tedious; annoying.

monotonous Without any change or variety.

protracted Long, drawn-out.

tedious Long and wearying.

tiresome Wearying and irritating.

uninteresting Without interest.

wearisome Wearying; tiresome.

58 brave

adventurous Fond of dangerous, daring or exciting enterprises.

bold Displaying daring and vigor.

courageous Possessing courage; brave; valiant; showing no fear.

daring Eager to face risk.

58 brave (con't.)

enterprising Ready to try new, difficult or dangerous plans; courageous in starting projects.

fearless Feeling no fear; daring.

gallant Nobly brave; courageous.

heroic Displaying the qualities of a hero; nobly brave.

intrepid Fearless; very brave.

resolute Brave and determined.

stouthearted Bold; courageous.

valiant Courageous; nobly brave.

59 broken

burst Shattered or split, usually by pressure from within.

cracked Broken without separating into parts.

destroyed Broken; ruined.

fractured Broken; cracked.

shattered Broken into small pieces.

smashed Completely broken.

splintered Broken into thin sharp pieces.

split Broken or cut from end to end.

spoiled Damaged beyond use.

60 clean

bright Unclouded and clear.

polished Smooth and glossy.

shiny Bright and luminous.

spotless Perfectly clean.

stainless Without dirty marks.

undefiled Pure.

untainted Without stain or spot.

untarnished With no loss of brightness or luster.

61 clever

able Having the power or skill to do something.

acute Penetrating in intellect or understanding.

astute Keen; sharp-witted.

brainy Intelligent; clever. [Informal.]

bright Lively and quick to learn.

brilliant Outstanding in intelligence.

capable Able to handle most situations.

competent Able to perform a task required.

discerning Shrewd; acute; discriminating.

61 clever (con't.)

expert   Knowing a great deal about some particular thing.
gifted   Born with great ability; naturally clever.
intelligent   Capable of reasoning.
shrewd   Having a sharp mind; astute; discriminating.
skilled   Thoroughly trained and expert.
skillful   Able to perform very well.
smart   Intelligent; bright.
talented   Possessing great ability.
wise   Able to use experience and knowledge of many things well.

62   cold

arctic   Extremely cold; frigid.
bleak   Windswept, bare and cold.
chilly   Slightly but unpleasantly cold.
cool   More cold than hot; slightly cold.
freezing   Cold enough to turn water into ice.
frigid   Very cold; chilling.
frosty   Nearly freezing.
frozen   So cold that water has been turned to ice.
icy   Cold as ice.
raw   Cold, damp and bleak.
shivery   Cold enough to make people shiver. [Informal.]
wintry   Cold, stormy and icy as in winter.

63 dangerous

chancy   Uncertain; risky.
hazardous   Involving risk or danger.
menacing   Suggesting that something harmful may happen; threatening.
ominous   Threatening; foreshadowing evil or unpleasantness.
perilous   Dangerous; hazardous.
threatening   Suggesting that something harmful may happen.
treacherous   Safe-looking but dangerous.

64   dark

dim   Not completely dark.
dismal   Dark in a depressing way.
dull   Lacking clearness and vividness.
gloomy   Dark and depressing.
murky   Very dark and gloomy.

64 dark (con't.)

obscure   Difficult to see.
opaque   Not letting light through. Dark and dull.
overcast   Clouded; sunless. Gloomy.
shady   In shadow; out of the sun.
somber   Gloomy. Lacking color.
sunless   Without sunshine.
unlit   Without light.

65   dead

deceased   Dead.
defunct   Dead; extinct.
extinct   No longer in existence. No longer active.
inanimate   Without life.
late   Recently dead.
lifeless   Without life.
moribund   Dying.

66   deep

bottomless   Having no bottom or end.
fathomless   Too deep to be measured.
profound   Very deep.
unplumbed   Of unknown depth.

67   dirty

bedraggled   Soiled and wet.
dingy   Shabby and dull looking; tinged with dirt.
dusty   Covered with dust.
filthy   In a very dirty condition.
foul   Offensively dirty and smelly.
grimy   Having ingrained dirt.
messy   Dirty and untidy.
mucky   Wet and extremely dirty.
muddy   Covered with mud or very wet earth.
slovenly   Careless and dirty in appearance.
smoky   Darkened by smoke.
soiled   Dirty; unclean.
sooty   Marked by soot.
squalid   Dirty and miserable. Degraded.
stained   Marked by stains.
tarnished   Dirtied and dulled by exposure to air.
unclean   Dirty; soiled.

68   dry

arid   Very dry and lifeless.
crisp   Dry and easily broken.
dehydrated   Having no water content.
desiccated   Thoroughly dried; dehydrated.
parched   In a waterless condition; dried up with the heat.
thirsty   Strongly desiring a drink.
waterless   Without water.

69   easy

convenient   Handy and suitable.
effortless   Requiring no effort.
facile   Easily, almost carelessly done.
manageable   Can be managed. Governable.
painless   Causing no pain.
simple   Uncomplicated. Easy.
undemanding   Making no demands of effort, time or thought.
yielding   Not resisting; submissive; giving way under pressure.

70   empty

bare   Empty. Without covering; naked.
blank   (a) Unmarked, as a page in a book.
         (b) Expressionless, as a person's face.
deserted   Abandoned; without inhabitants.
hollow   Having the inside empty.
uninhabited   With no one living there.
unoccupied   Without inhabitants.
vacant   Not occupied; empty.
void   (a) Empty; vacant.
       (b) Without force or effect in law.

71   exciting

arresting   Catching the attention; striking.
dramatic   Full of action or feeling, as in a motion picture or
       play.
fascinating   Attracting very strongly; enchanting.
gripping   Strongly holding interest.
interesting   Arousing interest.
sensational   Causing great excitement.
stimulating   Causing increased interest or action.
striking   Catching the attention.

71 exciting (con't.)

thrilling   Giving a shivering, excited feeling.

72   famous

celebrated   Well-known and honored.

distinguished   Well-known; famous. Having the appearance of an important person.

eminent   Prominent; outstanding; exalted.

immortal   Known throughout all future ages; undying.

infamous   Of bad reputation.

notable   Worth notice.

noted   Well-known and honored.

notorious   Widely known for evil deeds.

renowned   Well-known.

reputable   Well thought of.

73   fast

fleet   Swift; rapid.

hasty   Too quick for carefulness.

hurried   Hasty; done in a hurry.

lively   Moving with vigor and energy.

nimble   Active and agile; quick-moving.

prompt   Done immediately or at once.

quick   Fast; rapid; speedy.

rapid   Swift; speedy; quick.

speedy   Rapid; swift.

swift   Rapid; speedy.

74   fat

buxom   Plump in an attractive way.

chubby   Round and plump.

corpulent   Stout; fat.

heavy   Of great weight.

obese   Extremely overweight; very fat.

overweight   Heavier than one should be.

plump   Pleasantly stout.

portly   Stout; corpulent.

potbellied   Having a protruding belly.

stout   Plump; corpulent; somewhat overweight.

75   full

brimful   Full to the top.

75 full (con't.)

brimming Full to the very top.
bulging Swelling outward.
crammed Filled too full.
overflowing Running over the edge.
replete Abundantly supplied; filled.
saturated Containing as much liquid as can be absorbed.

76 happy

blissful Full of supreme happiness.
cheerful Full of cheer; joyful; glad.
content Satisfied; pleased; easy in mind.
contented Satisfied; pleased; easy in mind.
delighted Intensely happy.
elated In high spirits.
glad Happy; pleased; in good spirits.
joyful Glad; happy; showing joy.
joyous Joyful; glad.
merry Full of fun; joyful.
optimistic Hoping for the best; looking on the bright side of things.
pleased Feeling pleasure; satisfied; content.
satisfied Wanting nothing more.

77 hard

arduous Calling for great effort.
demanding Calling for effort, strength or intelligence.
difficult (a) Hard to do or understand.
            (b) Hard to get along with or please.
formidable Hard to deal with. Hard to overcome.
laborious Requiring a great deal of work or effort.
onerous Burdensome; oppressive.

78 hot

blistering Burning hot.
burning Hot enough to cause burns; glowing.
feverish Having a fever.
oppressive Sultry, heavy and exhaustingly hot.
red hot Heated to glowing.
scalding Hot enough in liquid form to cause blisters.
scorching Hot enough to burn slightly.
sizzling Burning with a hissing sound.

78 hot (con't.)

stifling Hot and airless.
sultry Hot and humid.
sweltering Oppressively hot, causing sweating.
torrid Hot enough to dry up and scorch.
tropical Very hot, as in the tropics.

79 hungry

famished Very hungry.
peckish Slightly hungry.
ravenous Extremely hungry.
starving Likely to die of hunger.

80 ill

ailing Sickly; unwell.
bedridden Confined to bed because of illness.
feverish With a high temperature.
indisposed Slightly ill.
mortally ill Fatally ill; ill to the point of death.
poorly In bad health. [Informal.]
sick Having some disease; ill.
sickly Often sick; not healthy.

81 last

concluding Bringing to an end.
extreme At the furthest limit.
final Coming at the end.
hindmost At the end of a line.
rear At the back.
terminal At the end; forming the end part.

82 late

behindhand Late with some task or appointment.
belated Overdue; behind time.
dilatory Not prompt; tending to delay.
last minute At the latest possible time.
overdue Later than the appointed time.
tardy Behind time; late.
unpunctual Overdue; not on time; late.

83 lazy

idle Inactive; avoiding effort.

83 lazy (con't.)

indolent Lazy; disliking work.
slack Slow and careless.
slothful Lazy and unwilling to make an effort.

84 light (i)

bright Having much light.
brilliant Sparkling and dazzling.
dazzling Giving off a bewildering brightness.
fiery Giving off a burning glow.
glistening Looking wet and shiny.
glittering Shining brightly at rapid intervals; brilliant.
incandescent Glowing with heat; intensely bright; brilliant.
luminous Giving off light.
radiant Sending out rays of light; shining; bright; beaming.
shiny Bright and luminous.
sparkling Shining brightly in small flashes.

85 light (ii)

airy Light as air.
buoyant Light enought to float.
featherweight Very light.
feathery Light; flimsy. Almost without weight.
portable Light enough to be carried.
weightless Without weight.

86 little

dwarf Much smaller than usual for its kind.
microscopic Too small to be seen except through a
    microscope.
midget Very much smaller than usual for its kind.
miniature Represented or made on a very small scale; tiny.
minute Very tiny.
pint-sized Small; made on a small scale. [Informal.]
pocket-sized Small enough to fit into a pocket.
small Little.
tiny Very small.
wee Very small.

87 more

additional Added; extra; more.
extra Beyond what is usual, expected or needed.
further To a greater extent. More.
increased Made larger, greater or more numerous.

88 near

adjacent Situated near or close. Adjoining.
adjoining Attached; bordering.
approaching Coming close to.
handy Easy to reach; convenient.
local In the neighboring area.
nearby Near; neighboring.
neighboring Near; bordering; adjoining.
next Nearest in time, order or position.

89 new

brand-new Fresh from the manufacturer.
fresh Recently produced or made.
modern Up-to-date.
newfangled Lately come into fashion; of a new kind.
novel Not known before.
original Made or expressed for the first time.
recent In the near past.
up-to-date Extending to the present time; modern.

90 nice

agreeable Pleasant and comfortable.
amusing Pleasantly entertaining.
attractive Likable; winning attention and liking.
charming Delightful and attractive.
cheering Giving joy, encouragement and comfort.
comfortable Giving comfort, ease or freedom from pain.
delightful Giving great pleasure.
enjoyable Giving enjoyment.
glorious Magnificent; splendid.
gratifying Giving pleasure or satisfaction.
pleasant Giving pleasure.
pleasing Giving pleasure.
refreshing Pleasantly different or new.
restful Giving an impression of peace and quiet.
satisfying Completely fulfilling needs or wishes.

91 old

aged Of a great age; old.
ancient Of very great age.
antiquated Old-fashioned; out-of-date.

91 old (con't.)

antique (a) Valued for age.

(b) From long ago or ancient times.

elderly Rather old; near old age.

historical Of interest because of its place in the past.

medieval Belonging to the period of the Middle Ages.

mythological Relating to ancient myth.

old-fashioned Out-of-date.

prehistoric Before recorded history.

traditional Handed down by tradition; customary.

venerable Respected and honored because of age.

92 open

accessible Easy to get at or into.

ajar Barely open.

gaping Wide open.

unfenced Without a fence.

yawning Wide open; gaping

93 poor

bankrupt Unable to meet one's debts.

beggarly Fit for a beggar; very poor.

broke Without money. [Slang.]

destitute Completely without money or property.

hard up Short of money. [Informal.]

impecunious Having little or no money.

in want In need of money and goods.

needy Without goods or money necessary for life.

penniless Without any money.

poverty-stricken Very poor.

94 pretty

beautiful Very attractive to look at.

elegant Showing good taste; excellent; superior.

exquisite Very lovely and delicate.

fair Of clear and bright appearance.

graceful Beautiful in form and movement; pleasing; agreeable.

lovely Of attractive appearance.

neat Set out in a tidy way

ornamental Decorated to create a pleasing appearance.

picturesque Suitable in appearance to be the subject of a picture.

94 pretty (con't.)
splendid Magnificent; glorious.
stylish Smartly fashionable.

95 quiet

hushed Made silent.
muffled Wrapped in something in order to dull or deaden the sound.
muted Softened; quietened.
noiseless Without noise.
silent Without sound.
still Quiet and peaceful.
tranquil Peacefully still.

96 ready (i)

mature Fully developed or ripe.
prepared Ready for use.
ripe Grown and suitable for use.

97 ready (ii)

alert In readiness; on the lookout.
expectant Anticipating; expecting.
prepared Ready for action.

98 rich

affluent Well supplied with possessions and money.
flush Well supplied; having plenty.
moneyed Having money; wealthy.
opulent Wealthy; rich.
wealthy Rich.
well-to-do Having enough money to live well; prosperous.

99 right

accurate Strictly correct in all details.
correct Without fault or mistake.
exact Accurate in every detail; precise.
precise Accurate in every detail; exact.
true In agreement with the facts.
unerring Without errors or mistakes; exactly right.

100 sad

dejected Cast down in spirits.
depressed In low spirits.

100 sad (con't.)

disappointed With one's hopes and expectations not realized.
discontented Dissatisfied and unhappy.
dismal Gloomy; dreary.
dispirited Depressed; discouraged.
dreary Gloomy; dismal.
gloomy In low spirits; pessimistic.
grief-stricken In deep distress and sorrow.
joyless Without joy.
lugubrious Sad; mournful.
miserable Unhappy; sad.
pessimistic Expecting the worst.
somber Dark; gloomy.
sorrowful Sad.
unhappy Sad; sorrowful.
wretched Extremely unhappy; miserable.

101 safe

immune Secure from any danger.
impregnable Unable to be overthrown by force.
invulnerable Unable to be wounded or harmed.
protected Defended from harm.
secure Free from danger, fear or attack.
sheltered Protected from weather or danger.
shielded Given protection by some sort of screen or defense.
unassailable Safe from attack.

102 slow

deliberate After careful thought.
dilatory Not prompt; tending to delay.
gradual By slow degrees; little-by-little.
leisurely Calm and without haste.
sluggish Moving in a slow lazy manner.
snail-like Moving like a snail.
tortoiselike Moving like a tortoise.
unhurried Without any appearance of urgency.

103 soft

cushiony Giving soft support.
downy Soft; fluffy; like down.
flabby Soft; weak; lacking firmness.
fleecy Soft and woolly.
limp Lacking stiffness or firmness.

103 soft (con't.)
pliable Easily bent; flexible.
spongy Soft and absorbent.

104 strong

hardy Able to resist hardships.
herculean Very powerful; of great strength, courage or size.
irresistible Overpowering.
mighty Of great strength and power.
overwhelming Too great to be resisted; overpowering.
powerful Strong; mighty.
stalwart Loyal and courageous in the face of attacks.
sturdy Strong and reliable under pressure.
tough Firm and hardy.

105 thin

bony Extremely thin so that the bones show.
gaunt Thin and hungry looking.
lanky Awkwardly long and thin.
lean Without spare fat.
meager Spare; scanty. Thin; lean.
scrawny Excessively thin.
skinny Very lean or thin.
slender Thin; slight; slim.
slim Slender; thin.
spare Without spare fat.
willowy Tall and slim.
wiry Thin but tough and sinewy.

106 tight

compressed Squeezed closely together.
jammed Pressed tightly against.
stuck Unable to move in any direction.
wedged Immovably held in position.

107 ugly

forbidding Looking dangerous or unpleasant.
ghastly Hideously frightening.
grisly Horribly unpleasant.
gruesome Horrible; frightful; revolting.
hideous Exceptionally ugly.

107 ugly (con't.)

horrible   Causing a feeling of terror or disgust.
misshapen   Malformed; deformed.
monstrous   Unnaturally large and terrifying.
repellent   Causing a feeling of disgust; offensive.
repulsive   Causing a feeling of disgust.
unsightly   Unpleasant to look at.

108   warm

close   Warm and stuffy.
lukewarm   Very moderately warm.
mild   Not cold.
muggy   Warm and damp.
sunny   Warmed by the sun.
tepid   Only slightly warm.

109   weak

decrepit   Broken down and weakened by age.
feeble   Very weak.
fragile   Easily broken.
frail   Very weak and fragile.
infirm   Feeble; sickly.

110   wet

damp   Only very slightly wet.
drenched   Very wet.
dripping   Wet with drops falling off.
flooded   Covered with water.
moist   Damp.
saturated   Unable to absorb more fluid.
soaked   Wet through and through.
sodden   Thoroughly soaked.
waterlogged   (a) Thoroughly soaked with water.
                  (b) So full of water that it will barely float.
watery   Containing water.

111   wide

ample   Large; big; extensive; roomy.
broad   Of great size across.
expansive   Of great size and extent.
extensive   Spreading over a wide range.
spacious   Big; extensive; roomy.
wide-ranging   Spreading over a wide area.

112 young

adolescent Between childhood and adulthood.
boyish Like a boy.
childlike Like a child.
girlish Like a girl.
immature Not fully developed. Lacking sense or wisdom.
juvenile Youthful; young.
teen-age Of ages 13 to 19.
youthful Young.

VERBS

113   answer

acknowledge   (a) To admit that something is true or has happened.
(b) To announce the receipt of something.

echo   To repeat at once.

reply   To answer.

respond   To answer; to reply.

retort   To answer back angrily or sharply.

write back   To answer by letter.

114   ask

appeal   To ask earnestly. To apply for help or sympathy.

beg   To ask earnestly or humbly.

beseech   To beg; to appeal.

demand   To request with authority.

enquire   To ask for information.

entreat   To ask pleadingly and earnestly; to beg.

implore   To beg; to entreat.

inquire   To ask for information.

invite   To ask someone to be a guest.

plead   to beg; to entreat.

request   To ask for; to ask as a favor.

115   beat

conquer   To defeat; to overcome.

crush   To conquer completely; to subdue.

defeat   To overcome after a struggle.

overcome   To defeat; to reach victory.

overthrow   To remove by force from a position of power.

trounce   To defeat thoroughly; to crush.

116   begin

commence   To begin.

establish   To set up permanently; to found.

found   To lay a base for growth.

inaugurate   To make a formal beginning of. To install in office with a ceremony.

initiate   To start; to begin.

institute   To set up; to establish.

launch   To set moving for the first time, sometimes with some ceremony.

originate   To make for the first time.

117 break

burst To break apart violently from within.
crack To split without destroying the original form.
crumble (a) To break into very small pieces.
(b) To fall to pieces; to disintegrate.
damage To injure or harm.
demolish To pull or knock down into ruins.
destroy To spoil beyond repair or further use.
fracture To break.
rend To pull apart violently; to tear.
shatter To break suddenly into many pieces.
smash To break into pieces by a heavy blow or blows.
snap To break sharply across.
split To force or break apart, especially lengthwise.

118 build

construct To make by putting together.
create To make something that has not existed before.
erect To set upright; to construct.
form To give shape to; to make.
make To bring into being; to put together; to build; to form.

119 burn

brand To mark by the pressure of hot metal.
char To blacken with heat.
consume To destroy completely with fire.
cremate To burn to ashes, usually a dead body.
gut To burn out the inside of a building.
scald To burn skin and flesh by contact with hot liquid or steam.
scorch To burn the outside of.
singe To burn the outside slightly.

120 buy

barter To trade by exchange, using goods rather than money.
pay for To give money in return for goods or services.
purchase To buy.
swap To exchange.

121 carry

bear To carry.
bring To carry; to take along to a place or person.

121 carry (con't.)

convey To take from one place to another.

ferry To carry passengers or goods across a narrow expanse of water.

fetch To bring; to carry.

ship To transport or send by ship, train, truck or other conveyance.

take To carry or bring along.

transport To take from one place to another.

122 catch

ambush To wait in hiding and take by surprise.

capture To take and keep by force.

ensnare To catch in a trap.

entrap To catch in a trap; to ensnare.

hook To catch or fasten with a hook.

net To trap by catching in a net.

seize To take by force.

snare To catch in a trap using a noose.

trap To capture by a hidden device or trick.

123 chase

dog To follow or track like a dog.

follow To pursue.

hound To pursue ruthlessly.

hunt To pursue in order to capture or kill.

pursue To follow someone or something in order to catch up or overtake.

search for To look for in many places.

seek To search for.

shadow To follow closely without being seen.

stalk To hunt, keeping out of sight.

tag To follow closely. [Informal.]

tail To follow closely and secretly. [Slang.]

trail To follow closely and secretly.

124 choose

adopt To choose for one's own.

elect To choose someone from a group, usually by voting.

pick To choose from a selection.

124 choose (con't.)

select   To pick out by some standard.
vote for   To choose by voting.

125   clean

bathe   To wash a person or animal all over.
cleanse   To make clean or pure.
dry-clean   To clean with chemicals rather than water.
launder   To wash and iron linen and clothes.
mop   To clean or wipe with a mop.
purify   To make free of unwanted substances.
rinse   To wash out with water.
scour   To clean by rubbing with some rough surface or
      powder.
scrub   To rub vigorously with brush, soap and water.
shampoo   To wash by rubbing with a soap-like liquid.
sponge   To clean or wipe with a sponge or damp cloth.
spring clean   To clean a room or house with extra
      thoroughness, usually after winter.
wash   To clean with soap and water.

126   close

bolt   To fasten with a sliding rod (usually a door or window).
lock   To fasten shut using a lock and key.
seal   To shut up and close, as with an envelope.
secure   To close and make safe.
shut   To close.
slam   To shut violently and noisily.

127   copy

ape   To imitate, especially mockingly.
duplicate   To make one or more exact copies.
echo   To repeat sounds at once.
emulate   To try to equal or excel.
forge   To copy for a criminal purpose.
imitate   To copy very closely.
impersonate   To pretend to be someone by mimicking his
      voice, appearance and manners.
mimic   To copy closely; to imitate; to make fun of by
      imitating.
mirror   (a) To reflect, as in a mirror.
      (b) To give a true description or picture of.
repeat   To do or say something again.
reproduce   To repeat, copying exactly.

127 copy (con't.)

trace To draw on a thin covering sheet the lines seen on a picture beneath.

128 cry

blubber To weep more noisily than necessary.
howl To weep with drawn out cries of rage or pain.
shed tears To cry; to weep.
sob To weep in a gasping way.
wail To weep with long cries of grief.
weep To cry; to shed tears.
whimper To cry feebly.

129 cut

chop To cut, usually by striking with an axe or knife.
cleave To cut in two; to split.
fell To cut down and bring to the ground.
gash To make a long deep cut.
graze To scrape or scratch a surface or skin.
hack To cut or chop roughly, especially with an axe.
hew To cut down or cut into shape with an axe.
lacerate To tear roughly; to mangle.
mangle To cut or tear roughly.
saw To cut using a tool with a toothed edge.
sever To separate by cutting.
skin To remove the outer coat or skin by cutting and pulling.
slash To make long cuts by striking fiercely.
slice To cut into thin strips.
slit To make a long clean cut or tear.
sunder To separate; to part; to sever.

130 dig

burrow To dig a hole in the ground, usually for shelter or refuge.
excavate (a) To dig out and leave a hole.
(b) To dig in order to find remains.
hoe To remove weeds from between plants by light digging.
hollow To dig a hole by scooping out.
mine To dig into the earth, usually for coal or ore.
plow To turn over the surface of the soil, usually with a plow.
shovel To shift earth, sand, coal or other heavy substances using a large scoop.
tunnel To dig through earth and rock to form a passage.

131 drink

gulp (a) To swallow noisily or greedily.
     (b) To swallow with difficulty.
guzzle To swallow greedily in large quantities.
quaff To drink freely.
sip To drink in small amounts.
suck To draw into the mouth using lips and breath.
swallow To take into the stomach through the throat.
swig To drink in large amounts.
swill To drink greedily.
taste To try the flavor of.
tipple To drink alcoholic liquor frequently in small amounts.
toast To drink to the health or success of someone.

132 dry

air To remove possible dampness by putting out in the air.
dehydrate To remove all water, as with dried vegetables.
drain To cause water to run away.
evaporate To remove water by heating until it vaporizes.
hang out To hang up to dry in the sun or wind.

133 eat

banquet To feast in a magnificent style on a special occasion.
bolt To eat greedily without chewing.
devour To eat hungrily, like an animal; to consume; to swallow up.
dine To eat dinner at midday or in the evening.
feast To eat abundantly in a joyful way on a special occasion.
feed To eat carelessly, like an animal.
gobble To swallow in lumps.
gorge To eat greedily until no more can be eaten.
munch To chew vigorously and steadily.
nibble To eat in very small bites.
swallow To take into the stomach through the throat.
taste To try the flavor of.

134 enjoy

bask in To enjoy a pleasant situation.
like To be fond of or attracted to.
relish To enjoy keenly.
revel in To take intense pleasure in.

134 enjoy (con't.)

    wallow in   To live self-indulgently or luxuriously as in some sort of pleasure.

135   fall

cascade   To fall like a waterfall.
collapse   To fall down suddenly.
descend   To go down.
drop   To fall.
plummet   To fall violently straight down.
plunge   To jump downward (into or through).
sink   To move down slowly, usually through water.
slump   To sink suddenly and helplessly.
subside   To settle down or sink slowly.
topple   To fall forward; to tumble down.
tumble   To fall headlong.

136   farm

breed   To raise a particular kind of animal for certain qualities.
cultivate   (a) To make fertile and productive for growing crops.
          (b) To grow crops.
dig   To turn over the soil.
grow   To produce plants or crops.
harvest   To gather fully-grown crops.
raise   To grow something, usually crops or animals.
ranch   To work a very large area as a stock farm.
reap   To cut the crops of grain.
rear   To breed and look after animals during growth.
sow   To plant seeds.
till   To make fertile and productive for growing crops.

137   find

chance on   To find by accident.
discover   To find out for the first time.
encounter   To meet with or come across.
ferret out   To find by hunting.
find out   To discover after an enquiry.
happen on   To find by accident.
locate   To find the exact position of.
realize   To become aware of and understand clearly.
unearth   To dig up. To discover.

138 fix

amend To correct a mistake by altering.
correct To set right; to free from mistakes or faults.
cure To restore to health.
mend To restore to good condition or order.
put right To correct; to set right.
repair To restore to good condition or order.
restore To bring back to former condition.
set right To correct; to put right.

139 fly

ascend To go up.
become airborne To leave the ground at the start of a flight.
descend To go down.
dive To swoop steeply.
glide To fly using air currents for power.
hover To stay fairly still in the sky by use of wings.
rise To move upward.
sail To fly using air currents for power.
soar (a) To fly at a great height.
       (b) To fly upward.
swoop To fly rapidly downward, usually in attack.

140 follow
(i)

(See chase)

141 follow
(ii)

come after To follow; to succeed.
come next To follow in order.
ensue To follow; to come immediately afterward.
go after To fill in the place behind.
go next To follow in order.
succeed To come immediately after and take the place of.

142 get

achieve To reach or win after much effort.
acquire To gain possession of.
annex To take as one's own; to appropriate.
appropriate To take for oneself.
attain To reach; to achieve.

142 get (con't.)

corner To buy up the available supply in order to raise the price.

earn To receive as payment for work.

gain (a) To obtain by effort.
(b) To increase (possessions).

gather To get together from various places; to collect.

obtain To gain possession of.

procure To obtain after careful thought and effort.

reach To get to; to arrive at.

secure To get; to obtain.

win To gain something as a prize in a contest.

143 give

accord To grant a favor; to grant a request.

award To give as a reward for effort or achievement.

bequeath (a) To give or leave by a will.
(b) To hand down to posterity.

bestow To give as a sign of favor.

confer To give as a sign of favor or honor.

contribute (a) To make a gift in support of something.
(b) To send an article for publication.

donate To make a gift, often of money, in support of a cause.

grant To give in response to a request.

leave To arrange for a gift to be made after one's death.

present To give on a special occasion.

provide To supply for use.

render To hand over, usually as a form of duty.

subscribe To promise to give or pay a sum of money.

144 go

abscond To run away and hide from authority.

bolt To run away suddenly without warning.

depart To leave, usually for a journey.

elope To run away with a lover.

escape To free oneself from danger by running away.

flee To run away from a threat of danger.

leave To go away from a place.

move To leave, taking one's goods to another place.

145 hate

abhor To shrink from in horror; to detest.

145 hate (con't.)
abominate To feel disgust for; to hate bitterly; to loathe.
detest To hate intensely.
dislike To feel an objection or distaste for.
loathe To hate intensely; to detest.

146 have

keep To remain in possession of something.
monopolize To get or keep entirely to oneself.
occupy To hold or live in a place.
own To possess; to have as a belonging.
possess To own; to have as a belonging.
retain To continue to have.

147 hear

eavesdrop To listen secretly to a private conversation.
monitor To check a radio or television transmission by listening in with receiver.
overhear To hear by accident a conversation between other people.

148 help

accommodate To supply something needed, especially board and lodging.
advise To suggest what to do.
aid To help; to assist.
assist To help; to aid.
comfort To encourage and offer support.
counsel To advise and offer an opinion.
oblige To do a service as a favor.
reinforce To give extra help or strength.
stand by To remain loyal to.
support (a) To provide for the needs of.
(b) To give strength or courage to.
sustain To give strength or courage to; to uphold.

149 hide

camouflage To disguise in order to conceal.
conceal To hide.
cover up (a) To hide something by covering it.
(b) To conceal or disguise, especially a fact.
disguise To change in appearance in order to deceive.

149 hide (con't.)

    mask   To place a covering over, usually the face. To conceal.

    screen   To prevent from being seen.

    secrete   To keep in a secret place.

    suppress   To keep back so that no one else will know.

150   hit

    batter   To strike repeatedly with heavy blows.

    beat   To strike repeatedly with force.

    belabor   To beat vigorously.

    buffet   To strike with the hand or fist. To knock about.

    flail   To strike with a flail. To beat; to thrash.

    flay   To strip the skin from by beating or lashing.

    flog   To hit repeatedly with a whip or stick.

    hammer   To hit again and again.

    knock   To give a short sharp blow.

    lash   To strike with a whip or lash.

    pummel   To beat with the fists.

    punch   To hit with the fist.

    rap   To hit with a light quick blow or blows.

    scourge   To strike repeatedly wtih a knotted cord.

    slap   To hit with the open hand.

    smack   To slap.

    spank   To hit with the open hand, especially on the bottom.

    strike   To hit.

    tap   To strike lightly.

    thrash   To hit repeatedly with a whip or stick.

    thump   To strike with a dull blow.

    whip   To hit with a whip.

151   join

    ally   To unite for a common purpose.

    assemble   To put together from parts.

    dovetail   To fit together with projections that fit into openings. To fit together exactly.

    fit together   To put together from parts.

    fuse   To melt together.

    rivet   To fasten with a rivet or rivets. To fasten firmly.

    solder   To join two metal surfaces by melting a soft metal on them.

    unite   To join together as one.

    weld   To join metal surfaces by the use of intense heat.

152 jump

bound To spring upward or forward.
caper To leap or jump about playfully.
gambol To run and jump about in play; to caper.
hop To jump on one leg.
leap To jump over, across or up in the air.
plunge To jump quickly into something.
spring To move suddenly and rapidly.
vault To leap over, usually with the help of hand or pole.

153 keep

clasp To hold tightly or closely.
detain (a) To hold back; to delay.
      (b) To keep in custody; to confine.
hold To keep possession of.
imprison To put or keep in prison.
preserve To keep in good condition.
put away To put aside for future use.
retain To hold in one's possession; to keep back.
secure To tie up in order to hold in place.
store To put aside in a safe place.
withhold To keep back.

154 kill

decimate To destroy much of; to kill a large part of.
execute To kill as a punishment, usually after a trial.
exterminate To kill off all of a kind.
massacre To kill in very large numbers.
murder To kill a person after planning to do so.
put to death To kill; to execute.
sacrifice To kill as an offering.
slaughter (a) To kill very large numbers.
      (b) To kill animals or food.
slay To kill.

155 know

comprehend To understand the meaning of.
grasp To understand information fully.
identify To recognize or point out as being a certain person or thing.
realize To become aware of and understand clearly.

155 know (con't.)

recognize　To know from a previous meeting.
understand　To know the full meaning of.

156　love

adore　To love deeply. To worship.
appreciate　To realize the value or quality of someone or something.
care for　To have a liking or affection for.
cherish　To value dearly.
hold dear　To have a great liking or affection for.
idolize　To worship as an idol. To be extremely devoted to.
like　To be attracted to; to be fond of.
prize　To value highly.
treasure　To think of and treat as very valuable.
value　To think highly of.
worship　To love and admire deeply; to adore.

157　make

build　To make by putting together; to construct.
compose　To make up poetry or music.
construct　To make by putting together; to build.
create　To make something that has not existed before.
erect　To set up by building; to construct.
fashion　To make; to shape; to form.
invent　To make for the very first time.
manufacture　To make goods on a large scale, usually by machinery.
produce　To make; to bring into existence.
shape　To give a definite form to.

158　meet

assemble　To come together in a group.
cluster　To form a close group about someone or something.
congregate　To gather together.
muster　To assemble, often for a military purpose.
throng　To come together in crowds.

159　move

budge　To move a very short distance.
drive　To cause to move forward or backward under control.
eject　To throw or push something out.

159 move (con't.)

fly   To move in the air under control.
propel   To drive along.
sail   To use the wind as power for movement.
shift   To change the position of something.

160   need

lack   To be without.
require   To depend on for success.
want   To be in need of. To desire strongly.

161   open

break open   To open by force.
open out   To unfold. To expand.
open up   To open.
pry open   To force open with a lever.
uncork   To take the cork from.
unfold   To open out the folds.

162   pay

award   To give after considering merit.
compensate   To make up for loss or injury by a payment of
    money.
refund   To give back money.
reimburse   To pay back; to repay.
repay   To pay back.
reward   To make a return for something done.
tip   To give a small amount of money for service.

163   plant

grow   To plant and tend until fully grown.
sow   To scatter seed in a place suitable for growth.
transplant   To dig up from one place and plant somewhere
    else.

164   play

amuse oneself   To occupy oneself agreeably in some sort of
    game or recreation.
fool around   To waste time foolishly, but agreeably.
frisk   To run and jump about playfully; to frolic.
frolic   To run and leap about playfully.
gambol   To run and jump about playfully.
have fun   To enjoy oneself.
revel   To take great pleasure in. To make merry.

164 play (con't.)

romp To play actively and noisily.

sport To amuse oneself; to play.

165 put

deposit To put down. To leave on account.

lay To put down, usually carefully.

place To set down at a particular spot.

position To place on a particular spot.

put down To set down. To deposit.

set down To put down; to put in position.

166 rain

drizzle To rain in very fine drops.

pour To rain very heavily.

shower To rain for a short time.

teem To rain very heavily.

167 rest

lie down To take a reclining position.

pause To stop for a short while.

relax To stop straining.

repose To rest; to lie at ease.

168 rob

blackmail To get money from by threatening to disclose harmful secrets.

burgle To enter secretly and steal.

embezzle To steal for one's own use money entrusted to one's care.

hold up To rob using a weapon or threats.

kidnap To seize and hold a person for ransom.

loot To seize unprotected goods in time of war or other disaster.

pilfer To steal in small amounts.

pillage To rob by force on a large scale.

plunder To pillage.

poach To catch fish or game on another person's property without his permission.

raid To make a sudden attack in order to seize or destroy goods.

rifle To search and steal.

rustle To steal livestock.

168 rob (con't.)

steal To take something from someone dishonestly and secretly.

thieve To steal.

169 rub

buff To polish using a special soft cloth.

chafe To damage or irritate by rubbing.

file To wear down using a rough metal strip; to rub to smoothness using a file.

grind To wear smooth using a rough stone.

polish To make smooth and glossy by rubbing.

smooth To make a surface even.

wipe To clean or dry by rubbing with a cloth.

170 run

charge To rush violently against.

chase To pursue in order to catch.

dash To run a short distance suddenly and quickly.

flee To try to escape by running away.

gallop To run like a horse at full speed.

jog To move along at a slow bouncing trot.

lope To run strongly and smoothly in long strides.

scamper To run quickly with short steps.

scurry To run hurriedly with quick short steps.

sprint To run at full speed over a short distance.

trot To run along slowly.

171 save

extricate To set free from difficulties or entanglements.

protect To guard from danger.

rescue To set free from danger.

retrieve To recover after losing.

salvage To save from being discarded or from possible destruction.

172 say

affirm To state strongly.

announce To state publicly.

comment To make remarks about a subject.

declaim To make a formal speech.

declare To state publicly or emphatically.

exclaim To speak out suddenly and loudly.

hint To make a slight suggestion, usually indirectly.

172 say (con't.)

lecture   To make a speech of instruction or explanation.
mention   To speak or write about briefly.
observe   To remark.
orate   To make a formal and florid speech.
preach   To make a public speech on religious matters.
pronounce   (a) To speak; to declare.
    (b) To give a formal opinion or decision.
rant   To talk stormily and noisily.
rave   To shout angrily and wildly as if mad.
recite   To repeat aloud, usually from memory.
remark   To make a short statement or comment.
shout   To call out loudly.
snap   To make an angry sharp reply.
speak   To talk.
state   To say; to remark.
whisper   To speak, using breath only, to avoid being overhead.

173   see

behold   To see; to look at; to take notice of. [Poetic.]
consider   To look at thoughtfully with the intention of making a decision.
examine   To study carefully.
gaze at   To look at steadily.
glance at   To take a quick look at.
glare at   To look at fiercely and angrily.
glimpse   To catch sight of briefly.
inspect   To look closely and carefully into.
look at   To glance at.
mark   To take notice of.
note   To see and mark; to notice.
notice   To become aware of.
observe   To watch carefully. To note.
perceive   To become aware of.
recognize   To know something again when it has been formerly seen.
regard   To look at steadily. To watch.
scrutinize   To examine closely.
sight   To catch sight of. To see after watching for.
stare at   To look at with fixed, wide-open eyes.
study   To look thoughtfully at.
view   To look over.

174   send

broadcast   To send out a message over a wide area, as by TV or radio.

consign   To send by special arrangement.

dispatch   To send off.

mail   To send by mail.

post   To send through the mail.

ship   To send by ship, train or truck.

transmit   To send a signal or message from one place to another.

175   shine

blaze   To shine strongly and brilliantly.

dazzle   To blind for a short time by a glaring light.

flash   To send out a sudden, brief, bright ray of light.

flicker   To burn unsteadily.

glare   To give out a strong bright light. To shine so brightly that it hurts the eyes.

gleam   To shine out, not very brightly but steadily.

glimmer   To shine softly and unsteadily.

glitter   To shine brightly in small flashes.

glow   To send out a soft steady light.

scintillate   To sparkle; to flash.

sparkle   To shine brightly in small flashes; to glitter.

twinkle   To send out small rapid flashes of uneven brightness.

176   shout

bawl   To shout in a harsh rough voice.

bellow   To shout loudly or angrily.

chant   To shout together as a crowd.

cheer   To shout out applause and encouragement.

clamor   To make a noise of opposition and complaint.

cry out   To make a loud cry; to shout out.

roar   To make a long, deep, continuous noise. To bellow.

scream   To make a long shrill cry.

yell   To cry out loudly.

177   sing

chant   To sing a short simple song in which several syllables or words are sung on one note.

croon   To sing softly and gently.

hum   To produce a low tuneful sound with the lips closed.

trill   To sing with a quivering vibrating sound.

177 sing (con't.)

warble To sing with a trembling effect.

yodel To sing with frequent changes from the ordinary voice pitch to a much higher pitch, as the mountaineers of Switzerland.

178 sit

perch (a) To alight and rest.

(b) To sit rather high or in a precarious position.

squat To sit almost on the ground with the knees drawn up.

179 sleep

doze To sleep lightly.

drowse To be half-asleep.

hibernate To sleep through the winter.

nap To take a short sleep, usually during the day.

nod To be nearly asleep.

nod off To fall asleep.

slumber To sleep. [Poetic.]

snooze To take a short sleep; to nap. [Informal.]

180 stay

abide To stay; to remain. [Poetic]

continue To keep on; to go on; to go on with.

endure To remain firm despite difficulties.

last To remain in spite of the passage of time.

linger To stay on; to remain behind.

remain To stay; to continue.

stand To remain firmly in one place.

stand fast To remain firmly in one place, usually in spite of difficulties.

tarry To stay on; to linger.

181 stop (i)

cease To come to an end.

conclude To come to an end; to bring to an end.

end To come to an end; to bring to an end.

finish To come to an end; to bring to an end; to cease.

182 stop (ii)

bar To block; to obstruct. To forbid.

deny To refuse.

exclude To keep out; to shut out.

182 stop (con't.)

forbid To order not to do.

halt To put a stop to.

impede To hinder progress.

prevent To keep someone from doing something; to stop.

prohibit To forbid, especially by law.

183 take

abstract To take away; to remove.

appropriate To take for one's own.

clutch (a) To reach out quickly in order to grasp.
(b) To hold very firmly.

fetch To go for and bring.

grab To seize quickly.

grasp To seize firmly.

kidnap To seize and hold a person for ransom.

seize To grasp suddenly.

snatch To take away by sudden force.

184 talk

argue To discuss with someone who disagrees.

chat To talk easily and casually.

chatter To talk rapidly and thoughtlessly.

converse To talk generally with others.

debate To argue about a topic formally.

declaim To make a formal speech.

dispute To argue heatedly; to quarrel.

gabble To talk rapidly and meaninglessly; to jabber.

gossip To chat aimlessly about people or events.

harangue To make a long pompous speech. To scold.

lecture To make a speech of instruction or explanation.

mumble To speak indistinctly.

murmur To speak in a soft low voice.

mutter To speak in a low rebellious tone.

prattle (a) To talk freely and artlessly as a small child does.
(b) To talk foolishly.

preach To speak formally about religious matters.

rant To talk stormily and noisily.

scold To find fault with angrily; to blame at considerable length.

spout To speak loudly and affectedly.

whisper To speak, using breath only, to avoid being overheard.

185 teach

coach To prepare someone for an examination or contest. To train in playing a game.

educate To instruct and develop the growth of a person.

enlighten To increase someone's knowledge or understanding.

instruct To give knowledge to.

lecture To make a speech of instruction or information.

train To instruct through practice.

tutor To teach one person or a very small group.

186 think

consider To think something over.

contemplate To view in one's mind.

daydream To allow the mind to wander.

imagine To form a picture or idea in one's mind.

meditate To think about; to reflect.

ponder To think something over carefully.

reflect To think carefully about something.

187 throw

cast To throw outward, often aiming at something.

catapult To throw with great force; to hurl.

fling To throw wildly and without careful aim.

heave To lift and throw with great effort.

hurl To throw very strongly.

launch To throw; to hurl.

pitch To throw with care, aiming to reach a definite target.

sling To throw in a wild manner.

toss To throw aside or upward with a light quick action.

188 touch

brush To touch lightly in passing.

caress To stroke fondly in a loving manner.

contact To make connection with.

feel To sense by touch.

graze To touch or scrape lightly in passing.

handle To touch or feel with the hands.

manipulate To control or work by the hands.

press To put pressure on or push against.

rub To move with pressure over a surface.

scrape To rub or scratch with something rough or sharp.

tickle To touch lightly so as to cause laughter.

189 try

attempt To make an effort.
endeavor To try very hard against difficulty.
strive To make great and determined effort.
venture To make a daring attempt.

190 use

consume To use up by eating, drinking or burning.
employ To make use of; to use.
expend To use up.
exploit To make use of unfairly.
operate To be in control of something while it is in action.
utilize To make use of.

191 wait

dawdle To act or move slowly in order to prolong the action. To waste time.
hang around To linger or loiter.
kill time To pass time aimlessly; to use up time.
line up To wait in line.
linger To wait about, not wanting to leave.
loiter To wait about without a purpose.
stand by To remain alert and waiting.

192 walk

amble To walk at a leisurely pace.
hobble To walk with shortened steps.
limp To walk lamely.
lurch To walk with uneven and unsteady steps.
march To walk with regular rhythmic steps.
pace To walk slowly with regular steps.
plod To walk slowly and heavily.
prowl To walk stealthily, like an animal hunting its prey.
reel To stagger.
rove To wander.
saunter To walk with a leisurely or careless gait; to stroll.
shuffle To walk with dragging irregular steps.
stagger To walk very unsteadily.
step To walk a short distance.
stride To walk with long steps.
stroll To walk at ease and at a leisurely pace.

192 walk (con't.)

strut To walk in a vain important manner.
swagger To walk with a bold, rude or superior air; to strut.
totter To walk with short unsteady steps.
trudge To walk slowly and with effort.
waddle To walk with short steps swaying like a duck.

193 want

crave To want very much; to long for.
desire To want; to wish for.
long for To want very much; to crave.
require To want; to have need for.
wish for To want; to desire.

194 watch

behold To see; to look at; to take notice of. [Poetic.]
gaze at To look steadily at.
look at To watch; to gaze at.
observe To watch carefully.
pay attention to To take special notice of.
view To look at; to see.

195 write (i)

engrave To cut lines into a hard surface.
inscribe To write, carve or engrave on.
print To make lettering on paper.
scrawl To write in hasty, badly formed writing.
scribble To write hastily and carelessly.

196 write (ii)

chronicle To write the history of.
compose To write original poetry or music.
jot To write information in short form; to note.
note To write information briefly.
record To put down in writing.
report To write an account of some event.

ADVERBS
AND OTHER WORDS

197 afterward

after At a later time.
later At a future time.
subsequently In the time following.
thereafter After a particular time or event.

198 always

constantly In a way that does not change.
continually Over and over again.
continuously Without a break.
endlessly Without end.
eternally Without limits of time.
everlastingly Endlessly.
evermore Forever. [Poetic.]
incessantly Without ceasing.
invariably Continually the same; without change.
permanently Lastingly.
perpetually Over and over again; continually.
unceasingly Without stopping.

199 carefully

cautiously Taking great care not to make a mistake.
circumspectly Prudently; cautiously.
conscientiously According to what one thinks is right.
considerately Thoughtfully, taking others into account.
meticulously Very carefully and conscientiously.
mindfully Keeping something carefully in mind.
thoughtfully With careful consideration.
warily Fearfully; cautiously.

200 easily

effortlessly Without effort or strain.
freely Without holding back.
simply In a straightforward uncomplicated way.
smoothly Without any difficulties or snags.

201 fast

hastily Quickly, without proper care.
hurriedly Quickly, without proper care.
quickly Swiftly.
rapidly Quickly.

201 fast (con't.)

speedily Quickly.
swiftly Rapidly.

202 nicely

agreeably In a pleasant fashion.
delightfully In a delightful way.
enjoyably In a way that gives pleasure.
pleasantly In a pleasant agreeable way.
pleasingly In a pleasant enjoyable way.
satisfyingly In a way that gives satisfaction.

203 now

at once Immediately.
immediately Now; at once.
promptly Almost at once.

204 often

continually Over and over again.
daily Every day.
frequently Often; at close intervals.
repeatedly Over and over again.

205 slowly

leisurely Without hurry.
lingeringly Slowly, as if wishing to prolong an action.
sluggishly Lazily; without vigor.
unhurriedly Without any hurry.

206 so

accordingly As a result or consequence.
consequently As a result.
therefore For a particular reason.

207 suddenly

abruptly In a sudden and unexpected way.
hastily Quickly, without proper care.
hurriedly Quickly, without proper care.
promptly Almost at once.
unexpectedly In a surprising way.

208 then

afterward At a later time.

208 **then** (con't.)

at that time   Then.
formerly   At a previous time.
lately   Recently.
once   At some time in the past.
presently   A short time later.
soon   In the near future.
tomorrow   The day following the present day.
yesterday   The day preceding the present day.

209   too

additionally   In addition to; besides.
also   Too; besides.
besides   In addition to; as well as.
further   Moreover; in addition to.
moreover   In addition to; besides.

210   very

exceedingly   In a way that surpasses all others.
exceptionally   As an exception to a rule.
exquisitely   Far beyond expected standards; very delicately.
extremely   Reaching the limit.
intensely   To a very great degree.
quite   Very.
remarkably   In a way that is worthy of attention;
    outstandingly.
utterly   Totally; completely.

INDEX

adj = adjective
adv = adverb
n = noun

Words printed in **bold type** are key words.
The past tense of all verbs is given.

a

abhor abhorred 145
abide abided, abode 180
able 61
abominate abominated 145
abruptly 207
abscond absconded 144
abstract abstracted 183
abundance 32
accessible 92
accommodate accommodated 148
accord accorded 143
accordingly 206
account 49
accurate 99
achieve achieved 142
acknowledge acknowledged 113
acquaintance 21
acquire acquired 142
acute 61
additional 87
additionally 209
adjacent 88
adjoining 88
adolescent (adj) 112
adolescent (n) (boy) 10
adolescent (n) (girl) 24
adopt adopted 124
adore adored 156
adventurous 58
advise advised 148
affection 33
affirm affirmed 172
affluent 98
affray 19
after 197
afterward 197

afterward (then) 208
aged 91
agreeable 90
agreeably 202
aid (n) 25
aid aided 148
ailing 80
air aired 132
aircraft carrier 45
airy 85
ajar 92
album 8
alert 97
all 1
alley 43
allied *see* ally
ally (n) 21
ally allied 151
also 209
always 198
amble ambled 192
ambush ambushed 122
amend amended 138
ample (big) 56
ample (wide) 111
amphibian 2
amuse oneself amused oneself 164
amusing 90
ancient 91
anecdote 49
animal 2
annex annexed 142
announce announced 172
answer (n) 3
answer answered 113
anthology 8
antiquated 91
antique 91

belated 82
bellow bellowed 176
bench 13
bequeath bequeathed 143
beseech besought, beseeched 114
besides 209
bestow bestowed 143
big 56
bill 35
biography 49
bird 2
blackmail blackmailed 168
blackmailer 51
blank 70
blaze (n) 20
blaze blazed 175
bleak 62
blind alley 43
blissful 76
blistering (hot) 78
blitz 19
blubber blubbered 128
boat 7
bold 58
bolt bolted (close) 126
bolt bolted (eat) 133
bolt bolted (go) 144
bonfire 20
bony 105
book 8
bore *see* bear
boring 57
borough 14
bottomless 66
bought *see* **buy**
bound bounded 152
box 9
boy 10
boyish 112
brainy 61
brand branded 119

brand-new 89
brat 4
brave 58
break broke 117
break open broke open 161
breed bred 136
briefcase 5
brigand 51
bright (clean) 60
bright (clever) 61
bright (light) 84
brilliance 31
brilliant (bright) 84
brilliant (clever) 61
brimfull 75
brimming 75
bring brought 121
broad 111
broadcast broadcast 174
broke *see* break
broke (poor) 93
broken 59
broke open *see* break open
brotherhood 38
brought *see* bring
brow 52
brush brushed 188
budge budged 159
buff buffed 169
buffet buffeted 150
build built (construct) 118
build built (make) 157
built *see* build
bulging 75
bulky 56
bullion 35
bunch 16
bungalow 27
buoyant 85
burglar 51
burgle burgled 168
burn burned 119

burning 78
burrow burrowed 130
burst (adj) 59
burst burst 117
bus 11
bush 54
buxom 74
buy bought 120
bypass 43
byroad 43

c

cabinet 9
caddy 9
call 37
came after *see* come after
came next *see* come next
camouflage camouflaged 149
campaign (fight) 19
campaign (war) 53
canoe 7
capable 61
caper capered 152
capture captured 122
car 12
care for cared for 156
carefully 199
caress caressed 188
carried *see* carry
carry carried 121
cart horse 26
carton 9
cartoon 39
cascade cascaded 135
case 9
cash 35
casket 9
cast cast 187

castle 27
catapult catapulted 187
catch caught 122
catnap 48
caught *see* **catch**
causeway 43
cautiously 199
cease ceased 181
celebrated 72
chafe chafed 169
chair 13
chance on chanced on 137
chancy 63
chant chanted (shout) 176
chant chanted (sing) 177
char charred 119
charge (n) 40
charge charged 170
charming 90
chase chased (pursue) 123
chase chased (run) 170
chat chatted 184
chatter chattered 184
cheer cheered 176
cheerful 76
cheering 90
cherish cherished 156
cherub 4
chest 9
child (baby) 4
child (boy) 10
child (girl) 24
childlike 112
chilly 62
choose chose 124
chop chopped 129
chore 29
chose *see* **choose**
chronicle (n) 49
chronicle chronicled 196
chubby 74
chum 21

d

defunct 65
dehydrate dehydrated 132
dehydrated (adj) 68
dejected 100
deliberate 102
delighted 76
delightful 90
delightfully 202
deluge 41
demand demanded (ask) 114
demanding 77
demolish demolished 117
denied *see* deny
deny denied 182
depart departed 144
department store 46
deposit deposited 165
depressed 100
descend descended (fall) 135
descend descended (fly) 139
description 49
deserted 70
desiccated⸳ 68
desire desired 193
destitute 93
destroy destroyed 117
destroyed (adj) 59
destroyer 45
detain detained 153
detest detested 145
devotion 33
devour devoured 133
diagram 39
diary (book) 8
diary (story) 49
dictionary 8
difficult 77
dig dug (cultivate) 136
dig dug (excavate) 130
dig dug (farm) 136
dilatory (late) 82

dilatory (slow) 102
dim 64
dine dined 133
dinghy 7
dingy 67
dirty 67
disappointed 100
discerning 61
discontented 100
discover discovered 137
disguise disguised 149
dislike disliked 145
dismal (dark) 64
dismal (sad) 100
dispatch dispatched 174
dispirited 100
dispute disputed 184
distinguished 72
district 30
dive dived 139
dog dogged 123
dogfight 19
donate donated 143
dovetail dovetailed 151
downpour 41
downy 103
doze (n) 48
doze dozed 179
drain drained 132
dramatic 71
drank *see* **drink**
drawing 39
dreary 100
drenched 110
dried *see* **dry**
drink (n) 17
drink drank 131
dripping 110
driveway (n) 43
drive drove 159
drizzle (n) 41
drizzle drizzled 166

drop dropped 135
drove *see* drive
drowse drowsed 179
dry (adj) 68
dry dried 132
dry-clean dry-cleaned 125
duel 19
duffle bag 5
dug *see* **dig**
dull (boring) 57
dull (dark) 64
duplicate duplicated 127
dusty 67
dwarf 86

e

earn earned 142
easily 200
easy 69
eat ate 133
eavesdrop eavesdropped 147
echo echoed (answer) 113
echo echoed (copy) 127
educate educated 185
effortless 69
effortlessly 200
eject ejected 159
elated 76
elderly 91
elect elected 124
elegant 94
elephantine 56
elope eloped 144
embezzle embezzled 168
embezzler 51
eminent 72
employ employed 190
employment 29
empty 70
emulate emulated 127
encounter encountered 137

encyclopedia 8
end ended 181
endeavor endeavored 189
endlessly 198
endure . endured 180
engrave engraved 195
enjoy enjoyed 134
enjoyable 90
enjoyably 202
enlighten enlightened 185
enormous 56
enquire enquired 114
ensnare ensnared 122
ensue ensued 141
enterprising 58
entire (the) 1
entrap entrapped 122
entreat entreated 114
erect erected (build) 118
erect erected (make) 157
errand 29
escape escaped 144
establish established 116
estate 30
estimate 40
eternally 198
evaporate evaporated 132
event 22
everlastingly 198
evermore 198
everybody 1
everyone 1
everything 1
exact 99
examine examined 173
excavate excavated 130
exceedingly 210
exceptionally 210
exciting 71
exclaim exclaimed 172
exclude excluded 182
excuse 3

execute executed 154
expansive 111
expectant 97
expend expended 190
expert 61
explanation 3
exploit exploited 190
exquisite 94
exquisitely 210
extensive (big) 56
extensive (wide) 111
exterminate exterminated 154
extinct 65
extra 87
extreme 81
extremely 210
extricate extricated 171

f

fable 49
facile 69
fair 94
fairy tale 49
fall fell 135
famished 79
famous 72
fan 21
fantasy 49
fare 40
farm (n) 18
farm farmed 136
fascinating 71
fashion fashioned 157
fast (adj) 73
fast (adv) 201
fat 74
fat (big) 56
fathomless 66
fearless 58
feast (n) 34

feast feasted 133
featherweight 85
feathery 85
fed *see* feed
fee 40
feeble 109
feed fed 133
feel felt 188
fell *see* **fall**
fell felled (cut) 129
felt *see* feel
ferret out ferreted out 137
ferried *see* ferry
ferry ferried 121
ferryboat 7
fetch fetched (carry) 121
fetch fetched (take) 183
feud 19
feverish (hot) 78
feverish (ill) 80
fiery 84
fight (n) 19
file filed 169
filly 26
filthy 67
final 81
finances 35
find found 137
find out found out 137
finish finished 181
fire 20
fish 2
fit together fitted together 151
fix fixed 138
flabby 103
flail flailed 150
flame 20
flare (fire) 20
flare (light) 31
flash (n) 31
flash flashed 175

flay   flayed   150
fled   *see* flee
flee   fled (go)   144
flee   fled (run)   170
fleecy   103
fleet   73
flew   *see* **fly**
flicker   flickered   175
fling   flung   187
flog   flogged   150
flooded   110
flower garden   23
flung   *see* fling
flush   98
fly   flew   139
fly   flew (move)   159
foal   26
folk   38
folk tale   49
follow   followed (chase)   123, 140
follow   followed (come after)   141
fondness   33
fool around   fooled around   164
footpad   51
forbade   *see* forbid
forbid   forbade   182
forbidding   107
forest   54
forge   forged   127
form   formed   118
formerly   208
formidable   77
forty winks   48
foul   67
found   founded   116
found   *see* **find**
fracture   fractured   117
fractured (adj)   59
fragile   109
frail   109
freely   200
freezing   62

frequently   204
fresco   39
fresh   89
friend   21
friendship   33
frigate   45
frigid   62
frisk   frisked   164
frolic   frolicked   164
frosty   62
frozen   62
full   75
funds   35
further (adj)   87
further (adv)   209
fuse   fused   151

g

gabble   gabbled   184
gain   gained   142
galaxy   16
gallant   58
galleon   7
galley   7
gallop   galloped   170
gambol   gamboled (jump)   152
gambol   gamboled (play)   164
game   22
gaping   92
garden   23
garden patch   23
gash   gashed   129
gather   gathered   142
gaunt   105
gave   *see* **give**
gaze at   gazed at (see)   173
gaze at   gazed at (watch)   194
get   got   142
ghastly   107
gifted   61

gigantic 56
girl 24
girlish 112
give gave 143
glad 76
glance at glanced at 173
glare (n) 31
glare glared (shine) 175
glare at glared at 173
gleam (n) (light) 31
gleam gleamed (shine) 175
glide glided 139
glimmer (n) 31
glimmer glimmered 175
glimpse glimpsed 173
glint 31
glistening 84
glitter (n) 31
glitter glittered 175
glittering 84
globe 6
gloomy (dark) 64
gloomy (sad) 100
glorious 90
gloss 31
glow (n) 31
glow glowed 175
go went 144
go after went after 141
go next went next 141
gobble gobbled 133
gorge gorged 133
gossip gossiped 184
got *see* **get**
governess 50
grab grabbed 183
graceful 94
gradual 102
grant granted 143
grasp grasped (know) 155
grasp grasped (take) 183
gratifying 90

graze grazed (cut) 129
graze grazed (touch) 188
great 56
grew *see* grow
grief-stricken 100
grimy 67
grind ground 169
gripping 71
grisly 107
ground *see* grind
group 16
grove 54
grow grew (cultivate) 136
grow grew (plant) 163
gruesome 107
guerrilla war 53
gulp gulped 131
guru 50
gut gutted 119
guzzle guzzled 131

h

hack hacked 129
had *see* **have**
had fun *see* have fun
halt halted 182
hammer hammered 150
handbag 5
handbook 8
handle handled 188
handy 88
hang around hung around 191
hang out hung out 132
happen on happened on 137
happy 76
harangue harangued 184
hard 77
hard up 93
hardy 104
harvest harvested 136

hastily (fast)   201
hastily (suddenly)   207
hasty   73
hate hated   145
have had   146
have fun   had fun   164
haversack   5
hazardous   63
hear heard   147
hearse   12
heave   heaved   187
heavy   74
held   *see* hold
held dear   *see* hold dear
held up   *see* hold up
help (n)   25
help helped   148
herculean   104
heroic   58
hew   hewed (cut)   129
hibernate   hibernated   179
hibernation   48
hide hid   149
hideous   107
high seas   44
highway   43
highwayman   51
hill   36
hindmost   81
hint   hinted   172
historical   91
history   49
hit hit   150
hobble   hobbled   192
hoe   hoed   130
hold   held   153
holdall   5
hold dear   held dear   156
hold up   held up   168
hollow (adj)   70
hollow   hollowed   130
holocaust   20

hook   hooked   122
hop   hopped   152
horde   16
horrible   107
horse   26
host (crowd)   16
host (lot)   32
hostilities   53
hot   78
hound   hounded   123
house   27
hover   hovered   139
howl (n)   37
howl   howled   128
huddle   16
huge   56
hulking   56
hum   hummed   177
humanity   38
humdrum   57
hung around   *see* hang around
hung out   *see* hang out
hungry   79
hunt   hunted   123
hunter   26
hurl   hurled   187
hurried   73
hurriedly (fast)   201
hurriedly (suddenly)   207
hushed   95

i

icy   62
identify   identified   155
idle   83
idolize   idolized   156
ill   80
illumination   31
illustration   39
imagine   imagined   186

j

k

know knew 155

I

laborious 77
lacerate lacerated 129
lack lacked 160
lad 10
laid *see* lay
lakefront 47
land 30
landscape 39
lane 43
lanky 105
large 56
lash lashed 150
lass 24
lassie 24
last (adj) 81
last lasted 180
last minute 82
late 82
late (dead) 65
lately 208
later 197
launch (n) 7
launch launched (begin) 116
launch launched (throw) 187
launder laundered 125
lawn chair 13
lay laid 165
lay down *see* lie down
lazy 83
lean 105
leap leaped 152
leave left **(give)** 143
leave left (go) 144
lecture lectured (say) 172
lecture lectured (talk) 184
lecture lectured (teach) 185
lecturer 50

left *see* leave
legend 49
leisurely (adj) 102
leisurely (adv) 205
lie down lay down 167
lifeless 65
light (adj) (bright) 84
light (adj) (not heavy) 85
light (n) 31
like liked (enjoy) 134
like liked (love) 156
limousine 12
limp (adj) 103
limp limped 192
line up lined up 191
liner 45
linger lingered (stay) 180
linger lingered (wait) 191
lingeringly 205
little 86
lively 73
loathe loathed 145
local 88
locate located 137
lock locked 126
locker 9
lodge 27
log 8
loiter loitered 191
long for longed for 193
look at looked at (see) 173
look at looked at (watch) 194
loot looted 168
lope loped 170
lot 32
love (n) 33
love loved 156
lovely 94
lugubrious 100
lukewarm 108
luminous 84

lurch lurched 192
luster 31

m

made *see* make
mail mailed 174
main 44
mainland 30
maisonette 27
make made 157
make made (build) 118
mammal 2
mammoth 56
manageable 69
mangle mangled 129
manipulate manipulated 188
mankind 38
man-of-war 45
manse 27
mansion 27
manual 8
manufacture manufactured 157
manuscript 8
march marched 192
mare 26
mark marked 173
market 46
market garden (farm) 18
market garden (garden) 23
mart 46
mask masked 149
massacre massacred 154
massive 56
match 22
mature 96
meager 105
meal 34
medieval 91

meditate meditated 186
meet met 158
melee 19
memoirs 49
menacing 63
menagerie 55
mend mended 138
mention mentioned 172
merchantman 45
merry 76
messy 67
met *see* **meet**
meticulously 199
metropolis 14
microscopic 86
midget 86
mighty 104
mild 108
mimic mimicked 127
mindfully 199
mine mined 130
miniature 86
minor (boy) 10
minor (girl) 24
minute 86
mirror mirrored 127
miserable 100
misshapen 107
mission 29
mob 16
modern 89
moist 110
money 35
moneyed 98
monitor monitored 147
monopolize monopolized 146
monotonous 57
monsoon 41
monster 2
monstrous 107
moonlight 31
mop mopped 125

more 87
moreover 209
moribund 65
mortally ill 80
mosaic 39
motorcoach 11
mount 26
mountain 36
mountainous 56
mouthful 17
move moved 159
move moved (go) 144
mucky 67
muddy 67
muffled 95
muggy 108
multitude (people) 16
multitude (things) 32
mumble mumbled 184
munch munched 133
mural 39
murder murdered 154
murky 64
murmur (n) 37
murmur murmured 184
muster mustered 158
muted 95
mutter muttered 184
myth 49
mythological 91

n

nap (n) 48
nap napped 179
narrative 49
nation 38
near 88
nearby 88
neat 94
need needed 160
needy 93

neighbor 21
neighboring 88
net netted 122
new 89
newfangled 89
newsstand 46
next 88
nibble nibbled 133
nice 90
nicely 202
nightcap 17
nimble 73
nod nodded 179
nod off nodded off 179
noise 37
noiseless 95
notable 72
note noted (see) 173
note noted (write) 196
noted (adj) 72
notice noticed 173
notorious 72
novel (adj) 89
novel (n) (book) 8
novel (n) (story) 49
now 203

o

obese 74
oblige obliged 148
obscure 64
observe observed (say) 172
observe observed (see) 173
observe observed (watch) 194
obtain obtained 142
occupation 29
occupy occupied 146
ocean 44
often 204
old 91

old-fashioned 91
old master 39
ominous 63
once 208
onerous 77
opaque 64
open (adj) 92
open opened 161
open out opened out 161
open up opened up 161
operate operated 190
oppressive 78
optimistic 76
opulent 98
orate orated 172
orb 6
orchard 23
original 89
originate originated 116
ornamental 94
overcame *see* overcome
overcast 64
overcoat 15
overcome overcame 115
overdue 82
overflowing 75
overhear overheard 147
overheard *see* overhear
overthrew *see* overthrow
overthrow overthrew 115
overweight 74
overwhelming 104
own owned 146

p

pace paced 192
paid *see* **pay**
paid attention to *see* pay attention to
paid for *see* pay for

painless 69
palace 27
paperback 8
parable 49
parched 68
parish 30
parka 15
parsonage 27
partner 21
passion 33
path 43
patron 21
pause paused 167
pay paid 162
pay attention to paid attention to
  194
pay for paid for 120
peak (mountain) 36
peak (top) 52
peckish 79
penniless 93
people 38
perceive perceived 173
perch perched 178
perilous 63
permanently 198
perpetually 198
persons 38
pessimistic 100
pet 2
pew 13
phosphorescence 31
photograph 39
pick picked 124
pickpocket 51
picnic 34
picture 39
picturesque 94
pilfer pilfered 168
pilferer 51
pillage pillaged 168
pinnacle 52

public 38
publication 8
pummel pummeled 150
punch punched 150
purchase purchased 120
purify purified 125
purse 5
pursue pursued 123
put put (place) 165
put away put away 153
put down put down 165
put right put right 138
put to death put to death 154

q

quaff quaffed 131
quick 73
quickly 201
quiet 95
quite 210
quotation 40

r

rabble 16
race 38
racehorse 26
race car 12
radiance 31
radiant 84
raid raided 168
rain (n) 41
rain rained 166
raincoat 15
raise raised 136
rally 22
ran *see* **run**
ranch (n) 18

ranch ranched 136
rant ranted (say) 172
rant ranted (talk) 184
rap rapped 150
rapid 73
rapidly 201
rate 40
rave raved 172
ravenous 79
raw 62
reach reached 142
ready (for action) 97
ready (for use) 96
realize realized (find) 137
realize realized (know) 155
reap reaped 136
rear (adj) 81
rear reared 136
recent 89
recite recited 172
recognize recognized (know) 155
recognize recognized (see) 173
record recorded 196
rectory 27
red hot 78
reel reeled 192
reflect reflected 186
refreshing 90
refund refunded 162
regard (n) 33
regard regarded 173
region 30
reimburse reimbursed 162
reinforce reinforced 148
reinforcement 25
rejoinder 3
relax relaxed 167
relief 25
relish relished 134
remain remained 180
remainder 42
remark remarked 172

s

safe (n) 9
saga 49
said *see* **say**
sail sailed (fly) 139
sail sailed (move) 159
salvage salvaged 171
sang *see* **sing**
sank *see* sink
sat *see* **sit**
satisfied 76
satisfying 90
satisfyingly 202
saturated (full) 75
saturated (wet) 110
saunter sauntered 192
save saved 171
saw sawed (cut) 129
saw *see* see
sawed *see* saw (cut)
say said 172
scald scalded 119
scalding 78
scamper scampered 170
schoolbag 5
schoolboy 10
schoolgirl 24
schooner 7
scintillate scintillated 175
scold scolded 184
scorch scorched 119
scorching 78
scour scoured 125
scourge scourged 150
scrap 19
scrape scraped 188
scrawl scrawled 195
scrawny 105
scream (n) 37
scream screamed 176
screech 37
screen screened 149
scribble scribbled 195

scrimmage 19
scrub (n) 54
scrub scrubbed 125
scrutinize scrutinized 173
scuffle 19
scurry scurried 170
sea 44
seal sealed 126
search for searched for 123
seashore 47
seat 13
secrete secreted 149
secure (adj) 101
secure secured (close) 126
secure secured (get) 142
secure secured (keep) 153
sedan 12
see saw 173
seek sought 123
seize seized (catch) 122
seize seized (take) 183
select selected 124
self-service store 46
send sent 174
sensational 71
sent *see* **send**
serial 49
service 25
set down set down 165
set right set right 138
settee 13
settle 13
sever severed 129
shack 27
shadow shadowed (chase) 123
shady 64
shampoo shampooed 125
shape shaped 157
shatter shattered 117
shattered (adj) 59
shed tears shed tears 128

snooze   snoozed   179
so   206
soaked   110
soar   soared   139
sob   sobbed   128
society   38
sodden   110
sofa   13
soft   103
soiled   67
solder   soldered   151
solution   3
somber (dark)   64
somber (sad)   100
soon   208
sooty   67
sorrowful   100
sought   *see* seek
sound   37
sow   sowed (farm)   136
sow   sowed (plant)   163
spacious (big)   56
spacious (wide)   111
spank   spanked   150
spare   105
sparkle (light)   31
sparkle   sparkled (shine)   175
sparkling   84
speak   spoke   172
speedily   201
speedy   73
sphere   6
splendid   94
splintered   59
split (adj)   59
split   split   117
spoiled (adj)   59
spoke   *see* speak
sponge   sponged   125
spongy   103
sport (n)   22
sport   sported   164

sports car   12
spotless   60
spout   spouted   184
sprang   *see* spring
spread (farm)   18
spread (meal)   34
spring   sprang   152
spring clean   spring cleaned   125
sprint   sprinted   170
squalid   67
squat   squatted   178
squeak   37
stagger   staggered   192
stained   67
stainless   60
stalk   stalked   123
stall   46
stallion   26
stalwart   104
stand   stood   180
stand by   stood by (help)   148
stand by   stood by (wait)   191
stand fast   stood fast   180
stare at   stared at   173
starving   79
state (n)   30
state   stated   172
statement   49
stay   stayed   180
steal   stole   168
step   stepped   192
stifling   78
still   95
stimulating   71
stole   *see* steal
stood   *see* stand
stood by   *see* stand by
stood fast   *see* stand fast
stool   13
stop   stopped (cease)   181
stop   stopped (prevent)   182
store (n)   46

store   stored   153
story   49
stout (big)   56
stout (fat)   74
stouthearted   58
strand   47
street   43
streetcar   11
stride   strode   192
strife   53
strike   struck   150
striking   71
stripling   10
strive   strove   189
strode   *see* stride
stroll   strolled   192
strong   104
strongbox   9
strove   *see* strive
struck   *see* strike
strut   strutted   192
stuck   106
study   studied   173
sturdy   104
stylish   94
submarine (boat)   7
submarine (ship)   45
subscribe   subscribed   143
subsequently   197
subside   subsided   135
suburb   14
succeed   succeeded   141
suck   sucked   131
suddenly   207
suitcase   5
sultry   78
sum (the)   1
summit (mountain)   36
summit (top)   52
sunder   sundered   129
sunless   64
sunlight   31

sunny   108
sunshine   31
supermarket   46
support (n)   25
support   supported   148
suppress   suppressed   149
surplus   42
sustain   sustained   148
swagger   swaggered   192
swallow   swallowed (drink)   131
swallow   swallowed (eat)   133
swap   swapped   120
sweltering   78
swift   73
swiftly   201
swig (n)   17
swig   swigged   131
swill   swilled   131
swindler   51
swoop   swooped   139

t

tag   tagged   123
tail   tailed   123
take   took   183
take   took (carry)   121
tale   49
talented   61
talk   talked   184
tanker   45
tap (n)   37
tap   tapped   150
tardy   82
tariff   40
tarnished   67
tarried   *see* tarry
tarry   tarried   180
task   29
taste (n)   17

taste tasted (drink) 131
taste tasted (eat) 133
taught *see* **teach**
taxi 12
teach taught 185
teacher 50
tedious 57
teem teemed 166
teen-age 112
teen-ager (boy) 10
teen-ager (girl) 24
tender 7
tenderness 33
tepid 108
terminal 81
territory 30
textbook 8
then (at that time) 208
thereafter 197
therefore 206
thesaurus 8
thicket 54
thief 51
thieve thieved 168
thin 105
think thought 186
thirsty 68
thoroughbred 26
thought *see* **think**
thoughtfully 199
thrash thrashed 150
threatening 63
threw *see* **throw**
thriller (book) 8
thriller (story) 49
thrilling 71
throne 13
throng (n) 16
throng thronged 158
throw threw 187
thud 37
thump thumped 150

thunderstorm 41
tickle tickled 188
tight 106
till tilled 136
tiny 86
tip tipped 162
tipple tippled 131
tiresome 57
toast (n) 17
toast toasted 131
toddler 4
tomboy 24
tome 8
tomorrow 208
too 209
took *see* **take**
top 52
topple toppled 135
torrid 78
tortoiselike 102
toss tossed 187
tot (baby) 4
total (the) 1
total war 53
totter tottered 192
touch touched 188
tough 104
tournament 22
town 14
trace traced 127
traditional 91
trail trailed 123
train trained 185
tranquil 95
transmit transmitted 174
transplant transplanted 163
transport transported 121
trap trapped 122
trawler 7
treacherous 63
treasure treasured 156
tribe 38

u

v

w

wail (n)   37
wail   wailed   128
wait   waited   191
walk   walked   192
wallow in   wallowed in   134
want   wanted (desire)   193
want   wanted (need)   160
war   53
war (fight)   19
warble   warbled   177
warily   199
warm   108
wash   washed   125
watch   watched   194
waterless   68
waterlogged   110
watery   110
weak   109
wealth   35
wealthy   98
wearisome   57
wedged   106
wee   86
weep   wept   128
weightless   85
weld   welded   151
well-to-do   98
went   *see* **go**
went after   *see* go after
went next   *see* go next
wept   *see* weep
wet   110
whimper (n)   37
whimper   whimpered   128
whine (n)   37
whip   whipped   150
whisper   whispered (say)   172
whisper   whispered (talk)   184
whole (the)   1
wholesale price   40
wide   111
wide-ranging   111

wildlife park   55
willowy   105
win   won   142
wintry   62
wipe   wiped   169
wiry   105
wise   61
wish for   wished for   193
withheld   *see* withhold
withhold   withheld   153
won   *see* win
wood   54
woodland   54
woodlot   54
work   29
worship   worshiped   156
wretched   100
write   wrote   195
write   wrote (compose)   196
write back   wrote back   113
wrote   *see* **write**
wrote back   *see* write back

y

yacht   7
yarn   49
yawning   92
yell   yelled   176
yesterday   208
yielding   69
yodel   yodeled   177
young   112
youngster (boy)   10
youngster (girl)   24
youth   10
youthful   112

z

zenith   52
zoo   55